JEREMY HODGES has been a reporter, feature writer, columnist and TV critic in a varied journalistic career stretching from Merseyside to Australia, John O'Groats to Glasgow. After writing his first article on Stevenson to mark the 1994 centenary of the author's death in Samoa, he developed an RLS obses-sion w                                                             ;ons in
Falkir                                                                y, with
every                                                                r more
than t

Please return/renew this item by the last date shown on this label, or on your self-service receipt.

To renew this item, visit **www.librarieswest.org.uk** or contact your library

Your borrower number and PIN are required.

D1513243

4 4 0004344  2

# Mrs Jekyll
# and
# Cousin Hyde

JEREMY HODGES

**Luath** Press Limited

EDINBURGH

www.luath.co.uk

To Christine, Tom and Jonathan for living with my obsession,
and to my parents for sharing their love of books with me.

First published 2017

ISBN: 978-1-912147-23-6

The author's right to be identified as author of this book under the
Copyright, Designs and Patents Act 1988 has been asserted.

The paper used in this book is recyclable. It is made from low chlorine pulps
produced in a low energy, low emission manner from renewable forests.

Printed and bound by Martins the Printers, Berwick-upon-Tweed

Typeset in 11 point Sabon by Lapiz

# Contents

# I

# Childhood Romance

FROM THE MOMENT it appeared, *Strange Case of Dr Jekyll and Mr Hyde* caused a sensation. The idea that a respectable professional man and a depraved monster might coexist in the same body – and that one might yearn to become the other – sent a *frisson* of horror through repressed Victorian society. Yet such was the skill of the story's creator that Mr Hyde's depravity was left to the imagination of thousands of readers, producing mental pictures more shocking than anything Robert Louis Stevenson might write. Clergymen even preached sermons inspired by such a highly moral cautionary tale.

Yet while the story that appeared in a lurid, cheap edition was devoured eagerly by the masses, those who bothered to read the dedication may have been puzzled to find the inspiration for Jekyll and Hyde was a woman. And nothing seemed further from the dark streets of London where Jekyll became Hyde and committed foul crimes than the accompanying heartfelt verses harking back to a shared childhood in Scotland:

> It's ill to loose the bands that God decreed to bind;
> Still will we be the children of the heather and the wind.
> Far away from home, O it's still for you and me
> That the broom is blowing bonnie in the north countrie.

Mrs Grundy, the mythological Victorian matron who stood guard over the nation's morals, would have been shocked to discover the woman to whom the verses were addressed was a mother-of-two who had left her husband and run away to France with another man. He might have been her cousin but Stevenson's attempts to save her from an unhappy marriage came perilously close to landing him in the divorce courts as a correspondent. Certainly the private letter he sent her along with a copy of *Jekyll and Hyde* would have seemed highly inappropriate from a man who was married himself: 'Here, on a very little book and accompanied with lame verses, I have put your name. Our kindness is now getting well on in years; it must be nearly of age; and it gets more valuable to me with every time I see you. It is not possible to express any sentiment, and it is not necessary to try, at least between us. You know very well that I love you dearly, and that I always will. I only wish the verses were better, but at least you like the story; and it is sent to you by the one that loves you – Jekyll, and not Hyde.'

The recipient of the letter, book and verses was Katharine de Mattos, daughter of the famous author's uncle Alan Stevenson. She and the cousin she knew affectionately as Louis had been close from childhood and would remain so until a bitter quarrel involving Stevenson's wife destroyed their friendship forever.

Katharine was born a year after her cousin, into the same engineering dynasty that built all the lighthouses around Scotland's coast. Their grandfather Robert Stevenson was immortalised by Sir Walter Scott as the builder of the Bell Rock lighthouse off Arbroath, and his work would be carried on by his three sons and two grandsons. But other descendants chose not to follow in his footsteps, including two christened after him – Robert Lewis Balfour Stevenson, never known as Robert but always Lewis or Louis, and Katharine's brother Robert Alan Mowbray Stevenson, known simply as Bob.

The Alan was mandatory in Alan Stevenson's branch of the family. Not only Bob but his three sisters – Jean Margaret Alan, Dorothea Frances Alan and Katharine Elizabeth Alan – bore both their father's names. Even their mother Margaret was known throughout the family as Aunt Alan. It was as if the name were in their blood, infusing it with elements of the dark, romantic, erratic and ultimately doomed genius that was Alan Stevenson.

Alan was his father's eldest son, born in 1807 and marked down early as a builder of lighthouses, although his frail health and inclination to become a romantic poet in the mould of Wordsworth indicated otherwise. At the Royal High School in Edinburgh, Alan was the most intelligent and gifted of the Stevenson boys and developed a love of the classics which continued when at 14 he went on to Edinburgh University. But at 16 he was asked to commit himself to a career and bowed to the inevitable, replying by letter to his father in roundabout, humorous fashion: 'I found in myself a strong desire of literary glory, and I pitched upon an advocate but there was want of interest. I was the same way with a clergyman; and, as I am by no means fond of shopkeeping, I determined upon an engineer, especially that all with whom I had spoken on the subject recommend it, and as you yourself seem to point it out as the most fit situation in life I could choose...'

After time spent in London, learning to become a gentleman, Alan applied himself to the business of engineering and the itinerant lifestyle it imposed, travelling from one construction project to the next around the coast of Britain. He was 26 when he arrived in Anglesey to work on plans for a new lighthouse at Point Lynas, and was invited to call at Llynnon Hall, the home of Welsh landowner Humphrey Jones. He and his Scottish wife Jean were happy to welcome a young man from her home city of Edinburgh – but there was a considerable social gap between the aristocratic Joneses and the Stevensons, still regarded as little more than gifted artisans. Mr Jones had qualified in medicine but had no need to practise as he owned a Caernarfonshire estate in addition to Llynnon, where he was Master of Foxhounds and a Justice of the Peace. When he and his wife detected signs of a growing affection between their young visitor and their daughter Margaret, it was not something they wished to encourage.

Yet the two had fallen in love and were determined to be together. The problem was overcoming the Joneses' objections to a marriage. Alan Stevenson, as he stood, was not good enough for their daughter. He would have to prove himself first. And so began an 11 year separation during which the young lovers pledged to 'save themselves' for each other until Alan's undoubted success enabled them to marry, long after the passions of youth were spent. By then he was 37 and she was 32, rather late to be starting a Victorian family, but their long-delayed union was soon blessed by the arrival of Jean, known as Mab, followed by Bob, Dorothea or Dora, and finally in 1852 by Katharine.

Alan Stevenson's family was now complete, living happily in Edinburgh's Royal Terrace, where he spent as much time with Margaret and the children as could be spared from his duties as Engineer to the Commissioners of Northern Lighthouses, having succeeded his father in 1842. By the time of his marriage Alan had proved himself by successfully completing Scotland greatest lighthouse, a 156ft giant called Skerryvore, 12 miles off the coast of Tiree. To achieve this feat he worked alongside the skilled labourers as they blasted foundations out of the rock and slowly assembled each precision-cut block of granite to form the tower. For seven days a week they worked long hours before collapsing on their bunks in a fragile barracks, bolted to the rock and hammered by storms until at times the men cried out in terror, convinced their time had come.

Alan, in a small compartment of his own, took his mind off the danger by writing poetry and corresponding with his friend William Wordsworth, who had come to value the intrepid lighthouse builder as a man of sound judgment in literature. Poetry had sustained Alan through his long years of separation from Margaret Jones, to whom he occasionally sent romantic verses. So occupied, he spent the six years it took to build Skerryvore, staying out on the reef each summer before the storms of winter drove him back to the comforts of Edinburgh. In 1844 the great light was lit for the first time and its triumphant creator was at last permitted to wed the woman he loved.

Yet their happiness was short-lived. No sooner was their family complete than Alan was struck down by a mysterious, paralysing illness. Bones ached, vision blurred and nerves no longer transmitted the power of movement. Scarcely had little Katharine learned to stand on her feet than her father lost the ability to walk beside her, and was forced to accept the life of an invalid. Slumped in a bath chair and swathed in rugs, he appeared like a spectre at the feast on what should have been happy family occasions.

In 1853 Alan resigned his post, his duties taken over by his brothers David and Tom. The rest of his life, through which according to family legend he 'lay on his face for 12 years until he died', was a forlorn pilgrimage in search of health, taking the family with him. For a while they lived in the Angus coastal village of St Cyrus, occasionally seeking out warmer climes in France, before finally retiring to Portobello on the outskirts of Edinburgh.

It was a sad, depressing life for the children, from which their natural high spirits found release when they were sent to stay with uncles and aunts. There was always a welcome at Uncle Tom and Aunt Maggie's home in Edinburgh, where Bob once stayed for several months. There he took refuge with his young cousin Lewis in a make-believe world where they were the rulers of two rival kingdoms, Encyclopaedia and Nosingtonia, whose affairs they would imagine in great detail.

In the summer, when the Stevenson families of Tom, David and 'poor Alan' would rent large villas in the country or by the sea, the two boys would be joined by Bob's sisters. Auntie Maggie, who could have no more children after Lewis, had longed for a daughter and always made a big fuss over her nieces. Bright, girlish and chatty, she was quite unlike their own Welsh mother who remained calm and impassive throughout her husband's long illness. But Katharine was less interested in discussing the latest fashions with her aunt than in sharing the make-believe adventures of her big brother and their cousin, both of whom she idolised.

At Bridge of Allan, near Stirling, there were long walks by the river to Dunblane, passing a small cave in the bank that was ripe for Lewis's 'supposings'. Who did they suppose might have lived there? Little did Bob and Katharine know that in their cousin's imagination the inhabitant of the cave would become a half-crazed, marooned mariner called Ben Gunn, immortalised in *Treasure Island*. Likewise the beach and rocky outcrops at North Berwick on the Firth of Forth were populated with pirates in the children's imagination. From dawn till dusk they could play on the sands, summoned occasionally to meals in the smart new villas that lined the sea-front. Uncle Tom and Aunt Maggie rented a large one in a row overlooking the East Sands and the Black Rock, on which the cousins would climb on their buccaneering adventures.

This was more convivial than the atmosphere at Anchor Villa on the West Links, where Alan Stevenson clung to life though an ever-darkening cloud of doom. It was not just nerves and muscles on which his paralysing illness fed. 'Poor Alan' was losing his mind. The Stevensons were all God-fearing people, brought up in the Kirk on which their beliefs were founded like the lighthouses they built, rooted to the rock to weather all storms. Before illness struck, Alan had worn his religion lightly and was happy to go along with his wife's Anglican ways, which in Scotland made his branch of the family Episcopalians. But as his affliction grew, he came to see it as a punishment from the Almighty for forsaking the true faith. Waves of guilt engulfed his mind as he cried out in terror, remembering how his men had done the same in the storms that battered Skerryvore. Slumped in his bath chair on the seafront, he was tormented by the thought that he had forced them to work on the Sabbath, the day of rest, in defiance of God's holy law. Later some of these workmen were puzzled to receive letters whose shaky scrawl implored their forgiveness.

For Katharine, Bob and their sisters, Alan's torment was deeply disturbing. It was hard for children to understand a father who, on Bob's 5th birthday, presented him with a bible inscribed in a fit of doom-laden religious mania:

> Read in this blessed Book, my gentle boy;
> Learn that thy heart is utterly defiled...
> This day five years thou numberest; and I
> Write on a bed of anguish. O my son,
> Seek thy Creator, in thine early youth;
> Value thy soul above the world, and shun
> The sinner's way; oh! Seek the way of truth.
> Oft have we knelt together, gentle boy,

And prayed the Holy Ghost to give us power
To see God reconciled, through Christ, with joy;
Nought else, but Christ brings peace in sorrow's hour.

How could children fathom the guilt that had turned the romantic poet who once penned sunny verses about Manuela the Mountain Maid into an angst-ridden penitent seeking to expiate his sins by translating the pious works of a 5th century Greek bishop into English verse as the Ten Hymns of Synesius? What sins could Alan Stevenson have committed that he felt the need to warn his innocent, five-year-old son about a heart 'utterly defiled'?

With modern hindsight, biographers have suggested that Alan Stevenson suffered from multiple sclerosis. In Victorian times, no such illness had been identified. In the minds of Katharine's uncles who shook their heads over the fate of 'poor Alan' – and perhaps in the tormented consciousness of Alan himself – the unspoken thought was that general paralysis was most commonly the result of syphilis. God's punishment on the fornicator could lie dormant for decades, long after the moment of lust and the briefly unpleasant symptoms of the initial contagious period. Then in mid-life *Triponema pallidum* might again rear its ugly head, boring into the bones with deep-seated ulcers, weakening blood vessels, enlarging the heart and destroying the nerves until the sufferer was confined to a bath chair by *locomotor ataxia*. As a final act, the disease might attack the brain, producing the ultimate Gothic horror – general paralysis of the insane.

For 11 years, Katharine's father had been expected to live like a monk before being allowed to marry her mother. In the barracks on Skerryvore, he had no option. But during winters in Edinburgh, where there were numerous brothels a stone's throw from his father's house in Baxter's Place, might the passionate poet have felt tempted to take a walk on the Hyde side? For countless respectably married Dr Jekylls and callow youths who adored sweethearts from afar, sex with a prostitute was a practical safety valve and did not really count as infidelity in the male mores of the Victorian age. But years later, paying a terrible price for fleeting pleasure, Alan Stevenson would never have been able to forgive himself for allowing his heart to be defiled by such wickedness, robbing little Katharine, Dora, Mab and Bob of a father's care when they needed it.

By the summer of 1865, the last act was coming to a close. From the house of gloom in Portobello, Katharine and Bob may have been glad of the chance to escape to the Borders, where Uncle Tom, Auntie Maggie and Lewis were spending July and August at Elibank Villa in Peebles. Katharine was 13 that summer, a strange, fey child on the brink of womanhood and falling shyly in love with her cousin. Louis might be painfully thin and at times in delicate health, but even in his early teens he had the charm that would win hearts throughout life's journey. Katharine might seem withdrawn and a little mysterious after years spent in the shadow of her father's illness, but she and Lewis understood each other and shared a passion for dark romance.

There was plenty to be found at Neidpath Castle on the banks of the Tweed. This once grand structure had been allowed to go to rack and ruin by its owner William Douglas, 4th Duke of Queensberry, whose decision to cut down the surrounding forest for the timber had provoked Alan Stevenson's friend Wordsworth to verses of condemnation: 'Degenerate Douglas! Oh the unworthy Lord!'

Since then the castle's west wing had collapsed, although one floor still served to accommodate a gamekeeper. When he was abroad, there was nothing to stop Lewis and the others exploring the mouldering, panelled rooms and narrow, winding stair to the battlements – where in a turret they chanced upon half a dozen back numbers of a long, romantic serial entitled Black Bess or The Knight of the Road. It was the work of one Edward Viles who, unbeknown to his young readers, churned out reams of lurid romance to support his addiction to alcohol and keep the horrors at bay.

The discovery of these 'penny dreadfuls' was doubly exciting for Lewis, as his parents would not let him read such stories for fear that they might corrupt young morals. The mildewed sheets were soon borne away to a nearby fir wood where the youngsters lay down comfortably on a bed of wild blueberries to read the adventures of the highwayman Dick Turpin at leisure…

> The rim of the rising moon was just peeping above the horizon, and a few faint, sickly beams of light shot up from into the night sky, giving to all objects a dim, spectral-like appearance. Standing in the middle of the high road which skirts Wimbledon Common on the north side was a horse and rider. The moonlight shimmered upon both with a strange effect. At first sight it seemed as though a lambent flickering flame was playing over them, from the horse's hoofs to the long feather in the rider's hat… He was tall and muscular and sat in the saddle with an ease and grace as rare as it was admirable… Of the steed which he bestrode, and which was no other than the mare so celebrated in song and story – Black Bess – we feel it is perfectly unnecessary to say a word in the shape of description. Her rider – whom we may as well at once call by name, Dick Turpin – had, at the moment we introduce him to our readers, one hand upon her neck…

Later the story portrayed its highwayman hero escaping from his pursuers across the rooftops of a city and appearing without warning through a trap-door into a room below:

> A horrifying sight met his gaze. Cowering on the floor, and divested of almost every article of attire, was a young girl of about 17 years of age. She was dark, and had long glossy hair hanging disorderedly about her. Her hands were clasped together tightly, and her face, under happier auspices, was doubtless beautiful, but now it was convulsed with agony. Her lips were apart and bloodless, and tears were streaming from her eyes.
>
> Standing over her, and flourishing a broad, heavy belt or strap, was a being in the shape of a woman. She was old and gaunt, presenting indeed more the appearance of an animated skeleton than aught else. Her eyes were bright and reptile looking, and a ghastly expression of delight and fiend-like malice lighted up her countenance as she struck the girl brutally with the strap. 'Help! Help! Save me! Save me!' shrieked the girl, as her eyes fell upon the newcomer... Dick passed his arm round the slight frame of the young girl and drew her towards him, endeavouring by this means to reassure her and calm her terrible agitation.
>
> 'Save you, my poor girl!' he said, in his deep, manly tones, which thrilled through every nerve of the girl's body with a feeling of exquisite delight which she had never before experienced, 'Of course I will...'

Victorian parents may have been right to deplore such literature, consumed so avidly by Louis and perhaps his shy cousin, who after years of lacking a strong male figure in her life may have longed for manly arms to hold her. Lewis for his part would always remember the holiday when 'that part of the earth was made a heaven to me by many things now lost, by boats, and bathing, and the fascination of streams, and the delights of comradeship, and those (surely the prettiest and simplest) of a boy and girl romance'.

For him, any fleeting adolescent passion would soon turn to fond affection. But it seems Katharine would always carry a torch for her cousin, although according to her mother's relative Ursula Wyllie, who used the pen name Susan Miles, it was Lewis who was first smitten: 'He was said to have been in love with Katharine. Whether she did not love him enough to marry him or whether the parents were opposed to marriage between first cousins I do not know. The man she did marry failed to make her happy...'

## 2

# An Unhappy Marriage

WHY KATHARINE EVER wanted to marry Sydney de Mattos was a mystery her family and friends could never fathom. The son of a Dutch East India merchant, he was a presentable young man who had studied law at Cambridge and might be thought to have good prospects, but he and Katharine did not appear to have much in common. She was creative, intuitive and artistic, living largely in a dream world, while he prided himself on an incisive, rational intelligence which led him to the obvious conclusion that God did not exist. There was no God other than William Sydney de Mattos and he would live according to his own moral law.

Nobody could have been less like Katharine's father, who had finally given up his life of torment just before Christmas. Alan's family had gathered at the house in Portobello and sat praying in the gaslight around the great lighthouse builder's bed as the obscene paralysis gently squeezed the last breath from his body in the small hours of 23 December 1865. It then fell upon Bob, now the man of the family at 18, to register his father's death.

Alan's widow kept the family together, supported by her late husband's two brothers who did their best to sort out his business affairs and make financial provision for his children, allowing Bob to finish his last year at Windermere College in the Lake District and go on to Cambridge. There he excelled as an athlete, gymnast and oarsman but achieved only a humble pass degree, without honours, in botany. Bob was a brilliant talker with an original mind, but it did not work well on paper.

His sisters were not expected to go to university but to make good marriages, and when they did so Uncle Tom and Uncle David would set up trust funds for them in their husband's names. As yet Katharine was too young to marry, and like other young ladies growing up in Victorian Edinburgh was kept in ignorance about sex. When her mother's carriage brought her and her sisters in from Portobello to go shopping in Princes Street, they would have no inkling of what went on in the dark closes they passed.

The grand eastern approach to Edinburgh had been built by Katharine's grandfather, cutting through a cemetery and requiring the removal of many bodies, including some of Robert Stevenson's own children who had died in infancy. Louis would describe the resulting thoroughfare as 'the New Town passing overhead above its own cellars; walking, so to speak, over its own children, as is the way of cities and the human race'. But it may have been more than his little dead uncles and aunts that caused him to use this curious metaphor. Just below the great Waterloo Arch built by his grandfather lay 'that sunless and disreputable confluent of Leith Street' where poor, half-starved girls barely into their teens might be trampled in the mire of prostitution.

Had Katharine stopped and looked down from the parapet, she would have seen the dark back-tenements of St Ninian's Row, lurking between the great arch and Leith Street. In her father's day this was known as 'the Sautbacket' or salt bucket, and may have been where 'poor Alan' absorbed the seeds of his paralysis. Here girls moonlighting from poorly paid day jobs as milliners, bookfolders or domestic servants could be had for a few pennies in the dubious privacy of tenement rooms which the part-time whores rented by the hour. No questions were asked and the respectable wives or sweethearts of the city's many Mr Hydes need never suspect anything amiss.

While Katharine knew nothing of Edinburgh's dark underbelly, her brother and childhood sweetheart were beginning to explore it. After enrolling at the university, her cousin had taken to spelling his name 'Louis' in the French fashion while retaining the Scots pronunciation, growing his hair and sporting a battered velvet smoking jacket. So clad, he would skip lectures and spend his days in an old public house that backed on to the Sautbacket, 'frequented by the lowest order of prostitutes – threepenny whores – where there was a room in which I used to go and write. I saw a good deal of the girls – they were really singularly decent creatures, not a bit worse than anybody else. But it wasn't a good beginning for a young man.'

At the same time Louis's father, as a director of the Edinburgh Magdalene Asylum, was endeavouring to save fallen women by offering them the chance of redemption through work in the laundry or sewing room while respectable married ladies read to them from the Scriptures. He would not have been happy to see his son consorting with the girls in their unredeemed state at 'Collette's', a subterranean shebeen below the old Sautbacket run by one Thomas Arthur Corlett, a Manxman of dubious origins with a murky, multiple marital history.

Admittance to this windowless hellhole below the pavement of Leith Street was by a door with a spyhole, at which Louis and Bob had to show their faces to gain entry. Inside, where the girls sought to pick up soldiers, sailors or medical students in various stages of intoxication, the cousins would rail against the hypocritical respectability of Edinburgh society. This was embodied in the mythological Mrs Grundy – although Bob preferred to blame her husband. In the sort of bizarre comic monologue reproduced later by his friend HG Wells, Bob would exclaim: 'Did I tell you of a wonderful discovery I've made? There's no Mrs Grundy. She's merely an instrument, Louis. She's borne the blame. Grundy's a man. Grundy unmasked. Rather lean and out of sorts. Early middle age. With bunchy black whiskers and a worried eye. Been good so far, and it's fretting him! Moods!

'There's Grundy in a state of sexual panic, for example – "For God's sake cover it up! They get together – they get together! It's too exciting! The most dreadful things are happening!" Rushing about – long arms going like a windmill. "They must be kept apart!" Absolute separations. One side of the road for men, and the other for women, and a hoarding – without posters – between them. Every boy and girl to be sewed up in a sack and sealed, just the head and hands and feet out until 21. Music abolished, calico garments for the lower animals! Sparrows to be suppressed – ab-so-lutely!

'And that's why everything's wrong. Grundy, damn him! stands in the light, and we young people can't see. His moods affect us. We catch his gusts of panic, his disease of nosing, his greasiness. We don't know what we may think, what we may say, he does his silly utmost to prevent our reading and seeing the one thing, the one sort of discussion we find – quite naturally and properly – supremely interesting. So we don't adolescence; we blunder up to sex. Dare – dare to look – and he may dirt you for ever! The girls are terror-stricken to silence by his significant whiskers, by the bleary something in his eyes…'

For Katharine sex remained a closed door without so much as a spyhole and she would never experience the Bohemian squalor of Collette's, from which Louis would stagger away long after midnight to his parents' home in Heriot Row while Bob set a course for Portobello where his mother and sisters lay sleeping. Having left Cambridge, Katharine's brother was now studying at the Edinburgh school of art. There the use of nude models provoked loud protest from Grundyite factions such as the Scottish National Association for the Suppression of Licentiousness, which campaigned to have the life classes banned as an affront to public morals.

Bob's response was to launch his own campaign of elaborate practical jokes to confuse and confound the city's upright citizens, in which his cousin took part enthusiastically. The two Stevensons invented a non-existent character called John Libbel, originally a pseudonym used by Bob when pawning a pair of trousers to raise the money for a train fare. To perpetuate the myth, they printed business cards for him which 'began to be handed about Edinburgh at a great rate, sometimes with manuscript additions which did not tend to improve the moral character of Mr Libbel'.

The crowning-point of the long practical joke was the Libbel Succession: 'Wherever we went, we had a notebook in our hand; we would put questions, look at each other, purse our lips, and gradually let it escape to our auditor, as if by accident, that we were agents looking for the heir to the great Libbel fortune. We tried to get an advertisement into *The Scotsman* newspaper, but the clerk plainly smelling a hoax, we were ejected from the office...'

Katharine might not have the freedom enjoyed by her brother and cousin but she would love to hear from Bob about the latest Libbel escapades and everything Louis had said and done. With two such colourful characters in the family, her own life did not feel quite so dull and constrained by Mrs Grundy. Travel, too, offered her an escape from the claustrophobic confines of Edinburgh, with visits to wealthy relatives in Wales and, increasingly, London with its array of theatres, museums and galleries that nurtured Katharine's love of art.

These were welcome distractions now that Bob was away in Paris, studying painting at the atelier of Carolus Duran. At the same time a tension had developed between Katharine's family and Louis's, which meant she did not hear from her cousin so often. Unknown to Katharine, Louis had been unwell with a disease that required him to convalesce in the spa town of Malvern, accompanied by his mother. From the symptoms it seems it was the same affliction that most probably caused Uncle Alan's sad demise.

Louis's parents had already accepted his refusal to follow in his father's footsteps as an engineer, so long as he studied law instead. They might now forgive his 'youthful indiscretion', as the quack remedies for syphilis phrased it. What they could never accept was his refusal to seek God's forgiveness for his unbelief. As part of his rebellion against Edinburgh respectability, he and his young lawyer friend Charles Baxter had invented a secret society called the L.J.R., whose initials stood for Liberty, Justice and, inexplicably, Reverence. Bob was a member, as was Louis's friend Walter Ferrier – a beautiful young man with an impeccable literary pedigree. A nephew of the novelist

Susan Ferrier, Scotland's Mrs Gaskell, he was also a grandson of John Wilson, who as 'Christopher North' had been a leading light of Blackwood's Magazine. To cap it all, Ferrier was descended from the poet and brilliant military commander James Graham, 1st Marquess of Montrose, known modestly as 'Scotland's Glory, Britain's Pride' – and Louis was in awe of him.

In such grand company, Louis had resolved to follow the L.J.R. credo, to reject the Established Church and 'disregard everything our parents taught us'. But on returning from Malvern he was confronted by his father with a copy of the L.J.R. constitution in his hand. On questioning his son, the God-fearing Tom Stevenson found Louis no longer believed in the Christian religion. The ensuing volcanic row lasted a year, with the family in Heriot Row convulsed by hysterics until Louis suffered a breakdown and was packed off to convalesce alone on the Riviera.

There his frustration at the repressive hypocrisy of Mrs Grundy's Edinburgh was aggravated further by news that the city was in the grip of a religious revival, led by the American evangelists Dwight L Moody and Ira D Sankey. From magazine cuttings sent out to him, Louis learned that James Balfour of Pilrig House, head of his mother's side of the family and a staunch supporter of the Edinburgh Magdalene Asylum, was one of those in the grip of religious fervour. This triggered an outburst of Hyde-like rage which Louis vented in a letter to Charles Baxter: 'I saw that bald-headed bummer J. Balfour had been describing a meeting he was at. He said, "They then enjoyed very precious and manifest tokens of the Lord's Presence." If I had been there and had sworn upon all the obscene and blasphemous phrases in my large repertory, that God had not been there, they would have told me it was because my heart was hard... O Sapristi! If I had hold of James B. by the testicles I would knock his bald cranium against the wall until I was sick.'

Meanwhile Tom Stevenson had been told that the Mephistopheles who had turned Louis into a 'horrible atheist' was Bob. In a highly unpleasant interview he told his nephew he never wished to see him again, and from then on regarded all the Alan Stevensons with mistrust. As if to confirm his suspicions, it then emerged that his niece Katharine had been seeing a young man down in London who was another callow scoffer at religion. Worse still, she had accepted Sydney de Mattos's proposal of marriage.

Louis arrived home from the Riviera towards the end of April, 1874, well in advance of the wedding. His parents had forgiven him and agreed to an allowance of £84 a year, enough to give him independence and membership of a London club. He agreed to return to his law studies that autumn, and in the meantime spent his days at his parents' summer home in Swanston, writing or roaming the Pentland Hills above the village. There he received bad news that threatened to wreck Katharine's wedding plans – Bob had returned from Paris and promptly gone down with diphtheria, which might easily kill him.

The house in Portobello, which should have been filled with excitement as everyone prepared for Katharine's big day, was filled with foreboding as the feverish patient's throat swelled alarmingly and Bob faced the prospect of choking to death. Louis was distraught and confided in a friend: 'This is the 6th case in my immediate family, whereof three have been fatal.' He went out to Portobello in fear that he would find the blinds down for a bereavement, but returned home euphoric in the knowledge that his cousin had safely passed the crisis point. Such was the sense of relief throughout the family that the rift was forgotten and Katharine was invited out to Swanston with her sister Dora.

Louis would tell a friend how he and the girls in the garden 'ended the afternoon by lying half an hour together on a shawl. The big clouds had all been carded out into a thin luminous white gauze, miles away; and miles away too seemed the little black birds that passed between this and us, as we lay prostrate with faces upturned. The similarity of what we saw struck in us a curious similarity of mood; and, in consequence of the small size of the shawl, we all lay so close that we half pretended, half felt that we had all lost our individualities and become merged and mixed up in a quadruple existence.

'We had the shadow of an umbrella over ourselves; and when anyone reached up a brown hand into the golden sunlight overhead we all feigned that we did not know whose hand it was, until at last I really do not think we quite did. Little black insects also passed over us; and in the same half wanton manner, we pretended we could not distinguish them from the birds. There was a splendid sunlit silence about us; and as Katharine said the heaven seemed to be dropping oil upon us, as honeydew – it was all so 'bland'... K, by the way, is just going to be married to an atheist, to the great horror of the family...'

That afternoon was Katharine's last intimate moment with her cousin before becoming a married woman. For better or for worse, on Thursday 25 June, 1874, she took Sydney de Mattos to be her lawful wedded husband. The wedding was at Dunblane, the scene of happy childhood holidays with Bob and Louis, and the ceremony took place at St Mary's. There de Mattos took wedding vows in accordance with the rites of the Scottish Episcopal Church, in which he had not the slightest belief, and his father and Katharine's mother signed the register as witnesses. Three months later, Katharine's Victorian sex education was complete when she discovered she was pregnant.

It had not taken long for her to realise she was unhappy with de Mattos, now working for a pittance for a law firm as part of his training. Without the income from his wife's marriage settlement they would have been struggling. Louis was one of the trustees along with Katharine's uncle, Humphrey Jones, but they had no say in what happened to the interest and dividends paid into de Mattos's bank account. It might be money from his wife's family, but he did not seem inclined to pass much of it on to his wife. This left Katharine so short of funds that she was desperate to have an income of her own, in an age where respectable middle-class married women were not meant to work. She knew Louis was starting to have some success writing for literary magazines that paid well, and begged him to help her learn to write. Ashamed to admit her marriage had been a mistake, she made no mention of her money problems when she sought his advice on something she had written, a disturbing description of a road running through a mysterious village.

Her cousin pulled no punches: 'Now, for the introduction. I am going to be rude. It's all bad. It is woolly, hard to follow, and disorderly...' But Louis could also sense what she was trying to achieve, even if it made him feel uneasy, like the more morbid tales of Edgar Allan Poe which he was reviewing for the *Academy* magazine. 'I shall never get the village out of my head,' he told Katharine. 'I know the place; it is called (to imitate Bunyan) the village of Hope-deferred, and near it goes the river of the Shadow of Suicide. I have seen the white faces at the upper windows, and heard the singing, and walked with the wayfarers; and I pray God (if there is such a gentleman) that I may come no more into that countryside: it is not wholesome for any long sojourn: it is a place to go through in a coach and four and never bait, or so much as draw bridle, till you are over the border again in better air and among more cheerful people.'

Had Louis known how desperate Katharine was feeling, pregnant and trapped in a loveless marriage, he might have kept the river of the Shadow of Suicide to himself. Instead, he confessed to his cousin how the religious rows with his parents that drove him to a breakdown had once made him think of ending his own life: 'And I say, you must not despond; however bad things are, you know they do come straight; when I think of the time when I wished to kill myself, for instance, and see the pleasure I should have missed, I am humbled at my own precipitate folly.'

The cause of Katharine's despondency was more than literary, but the advice he gave her was positive: 'You have to learn to write first a good deal better. Do you understand me, when I say you are writing with gloves on just now; you must learn to write with the quick of your fingers. If you persevere, you will learn, and well.'

Louis could already sense that something was the matter with his cousin, and was soon alerted to her problems by a letter from France in which Bob let slip: 'I suppose you have heard from Katharine about De Mattos. They do not get on together, I am sorry to say. He is a fool.'

Like the rest of the family, Louis was hardly surprised but responded: 'I am sorry to hear about Katharine. I did not twig it myself and she said nothing; but then I did not see them much and was not thinking of it much. The thing she has written is quite childish in style; but it is all right, and shows power; she will be able to write well if she has patience. Of course, one always knew De Mattos had no nerves, and was rather a braying ass; I never should have liked to marry him myself; and I'm damned sorry Katharine has, since it's come to that. It's awful depressing, like most things.'

# 3
# Glimpses of Hyde

SOON AFTER LOUIS learned of Katharine's marital troubles, she confided in her cousin that de Mattos kept her desperately short of money from her own marriage settlement. This was why she needed to write. Like the chivalrous Dick Turpin in the penny dreadful – 'Save you my poor girl! Of course I will' – Louis at once came riding to her rescue. Despite Katharine's lack of experience, he would find her some work reviewing books, giving her a small income of her own. To a friend he confided: 'I am sorely exercised about my poor cousin – the married girl – I have had a very distressing letter from her, praying for some immediate work that should remunerate – you can't tell (so she writes) you can't tell the difference it would make! Surely if there is one thing pure and lovely and of good report, it is to give women work. I think I shall manage for her; but not without throwing a good deal on myself. I am going to take service with a daily paper here; I shall read the books and make my own notes, and then send them on to her; she can then write what she will, I can always straighten it up when it comes back.'

Louis had built up a network of literary contacts since first writing for publication in a short-lived college magazine set up by a group of students including Walter Ferrier and a young Tory swell called Robert Glasgow Brown. The magazine soon folded but Brown went on to edit *Vanity Fair*. Meanwhile Ferrier's literary ability fell early victim to the demon drink, which would transform a witty, charming and original young man into a boorish, arrogant sot. While Louis's rows with his parents had been over religion, it was drink that estranged Ferrier from his family, until without warning he disappeared from Edinburgh and took alcoholic refuge in lodgings on the Isle of Wight. There, between binges, he struggled to write a novel. His late father's old publisher John Blackwood had agreed to consider the manuscript but had so far received only letters begging for advance sums, scrawled in handwriting redolent of *delirium tremens*.

Louis went on to place stylish if inconsequential essays with distinguished magazines such as the *Cornhill*, whose editor introduced him to another contributor then languishing as a charity case in the Edinburgh infirmary. Burly and bearded with a West Country accent but maimed by the loss of a leg through tuberculosis, William Ernest Henley would be the inspiration for Long John Silver. Soon he and Louis, skinny and boyish as Jim Hawkins, would be firm friends and collaborators. When Henley got out of hospital, they would spend hours in Edinburgh taverns discussing each other's work and sharing dreams of literary glory.

While Louis was forging ahead as a writer, Katharine found her life increasingly taken up with motherhood. In the summer of 1875 her daughter Helen was born in Portobello, where Katharine spent the last weeks of her first confinement in her mother's care. De Mattos now had an extra mouth to feed on his wages as a trainee lawyer, supplemented by the income from his wife's marriage settlement. Unable to settle to a career, he became speculatively involved as secretary to the Tinfoil Decorative Painting Company, offering an 'Economical and New style of Painting and Decorating the Interior of Houses, Churches, Theatres, Railway Carriages, and Yachts by the Patented Tinfoil. By this process it is almost impossible to discern the difference between it and real woods and marbles... Large mansions can be decorated in a few days without the removal of furniture, and there is also no smell of paint. It may be washed and cleaned whenever required, and the Tinfoil being damp-proof it is extremely suitable for new or damp buildings...'

Yet for all de Mattos's get-rich-quick schemes, he still kept his wife on short commons while denying himself nothing, including perhaps other women. Katharine, with a small daughter to look after, had little opportunity now to earn an income of her own but still nurtured hopes of a writing career like that of her successful cousin.

Meanwhile Walter Ferrier struggled on, through an alcoholic haze, to complete his novel. During his absence down south, his widowed mother had grown so desperate that she wrote to Louis, as one of Walter's less-debauched friends: 'My dear Mr Stevenson, As the mother of your friend Walter Ferrier, I am about to inform you of what you will feel grief and surprise at. This miserable victim, has just escaped Delirium tremens and has been indulging in a very terrible way in the Isle of Wight quite apart from his relatives and as usual deceiving those he has been with... he now exists among the number of those degraded ones whose society on earth is shunned by the

Moral and the virtuous among Mankind – Verily he will reap the whirl wind and who will stay him – his short note to me was but a formal wish that this New Year should be a better one for us all, knowing all the while that he was giving rein to his animal desire of drink... May a mother's affection so send me to my God in prayer but my heart seems drying up within me when I think of all that has been done for this son – My consolation is that his honoured Father is not here...'

Ferrier's 'honoured father' had died in 1864, the year before Alan Stevenson and apparently from the same disease. His wife Margaret, once known as the intelligent and witty daughter of 'Christopher North', was too innocent to realise the most likely cause of the paralysis that would confine her to a bath chair before robbing her of her life. Her husband, the eminent philosopher Professor James Frederick Ferrier, had gone down to London in 1853 to lobby Parliament on behalf of the University of St Andrews. During this business trip it seems he indulged his Hyde side with a visit to the Cremorne pleasure gardens, a notorious haunt of prostitutes, and disappeared with one of them into the bushes. A few minutes later, the already remorseful Professor Jekyll emerged with the syphilis that would cut short his life 12 years later. Tragically it seems he did not abstain from marital relations during the infectious stage, unwittingly condemning his wife to years of paralysis.

Katharine was perhaps lucky not to suffer the same fate. While her freethinking husband was inclined to extramarital sexual encounters, he still insisted on his conjugal rights and in the summer of 1876 Katharine discovered she was again pregnant. Yet the prospect of a growing family did not seem to instil a greater sense of responsibility in de Mattos, who had given up on a legal career and now earned a small income as a private tutor of mathematics, augmented by his wife's trust money. Pregnant and trapped in an unhappy home with never enough to pay the bills, Katharine's position was desperate. With plenty of time to reflect, she may often have wondered how life might have been had she been able to marry her cousin instead.

Louis, meanwhile, was in a canoe, paddling down the waterways of Belgium and France to meet his own romantic destiny. Her name was Fanny Osbourne. She was ten years older than him, and unhappily married to an unfaithful husband in San Francisco. Unable to bear the constant humiliation of Sam Osbourne's affairs with saloon bar whores, Fanny had fled to France to study art with her teenage daughter Belle, taking her two young sons with them. But in Paris little Hervey had fallen ill with a virulent consumption that racked his diminutive body with horrific haemorrhages until he died shortly after his 5th birthday. Filled with remorse, Fanny feared young Samuel Lloyd might suffer the same fate. Desperate to get out of unhealthy cheap lodgings in Paris, she had moved her little family to the Hotel Chevillon in the village of Grez-sur-Loing by the forest of Fontaine-bleau, where Bob Stevenson and his Bohemian painter friends made their summer headquarters.

There, in the autumn of 1876, Louis hauled his canoe out of the water at the back of the hotel in Grez and vaulted in through a window, to the cheers of his Bohemian friends. Across the room he spotted the tough little American woman who was his destiny, her dark eyes looking directly into his, like a man sighting a pistol.

Soon Fanny and Louis were inseparable, sitting smoking and sharing their life stories by the hotel stove while the artists were out sketching in the forest. Louis would have to return shortly to Edinburgh and the pantomime of pretending to be an advocate, but for the next two years he would spend all the time he could in France with Mrs Osbourne.

Naturally Louis's family could not be told about her. His parents would have been scandalised to learn their son had moved into the lodgings Fanny had taken for her little family in Montmartre, where sinfully he now shared her bed. In Edinburgh only Louis's lawyer friend Baxter and the piratical Henley were taken into his confidence about the affair. Apart from Bob, who already knew everything, the rest of the family were kept in the dark – including poor, pregnant Katharine.

For her there was at least a glimmer of hope when Henley secured his first job as an editor. Robert Glasgow Brown had parted company with *Vanity Fair* and had persuaded some wealthy Tory backers to finance a new publication called *London: The Conservative Weekly Journal of Politics, Finance, Society and the Arts*. After the first few issues, Brown had relinquished the reins to Henley – who was free to commission articles from any promising writer. Soon Katharine was finding regular work there, along with Louis and Walter Ferrier.

The young man once known to his friends as '*le jeune et beau*' had returned to Edinburgh a bloated wreck of his former beautiful self. Yet Ferrier had, against the odds, completed his novel, and Louis helped him go over the manuscript before sending it off to John Blackwood. Ferrier, his literary labours now done, bowed to family pressure and admitted himself to the drying-out ward at the Chambers Hospital. There he braved the ordeal of alcoholic withdrawal, perhaps alleviated by the bottle which his family and Blackwood suspected he kept hidden away to ward off the horrors.

The first issue of *London* appeared in the February of 1877, and five weeks later young Richard de Mattos was born. His sister Helen was now toddling about the house, her childhood curls kept tidy in a pretty little hairnet or snood which earned her the lifelong nickname 'Snoodie'. In other circumstances, with another husband, Katharine might have been blissfully happy. As it was, she had plenty of cause for postnatal depression and the feeling of being trapped was becoming unbearable.

Meanwhile, Louis's affair with Fanny Osbourne was growing steadily more serious, although he had the sense to stay away from France when Fanny's husband came over to visit his runaway wife and see his two children. When Sam Osbourne appeared at the door of their lodgings in Montmartre there were shouts of joy from Belle and young Sammy, as his surviving son was then known. Fanny may not have been so delighted to have her faithless husband moving into her bedroom, but Sam was still a handsome man and it was not easy to resist his charm – as many women in San Francisco could testify.

Yet if Sam made any serious attempt to rekindle their relationship, it was doomed to failure when they went out to stay at the Hotel Chevillon in Grez. There, for Fanny's sake, Bob and the rest of the Bohemian community did their best to tolerate the bourgeois American lothario who seemed incapable of keeping his hands off the local peasant girls. For Fanny this was the last straw, and she was probably relieved when her husband received a telegram summoning him back to California. His job there as a stenographer in the law courts did not pay enough to finance his lifestyle, so Sam had taken to speculating on the stock exchange, which was now taking a tumble. If he did not wish to see his get-rich-quick schemes turn to dust, he had to get back to attend to his affairs, financial or otherwise. Extracting a promise from Fanny that she would bring his family home within a year, he gave a grudging assurance that he would continue to send her an allowance, before departing for the delights of San Francisco.

This left the coast clear for the return of Louis, for a Bohemian summer of forest walks and boating on the Loing at Grez, where Bob and the other artists conducted mock 'sea battles' in canoes and washtubs. Fanny, desperate to escape her unhappy marriage and feelings of guilt over little Hervey's death, kicked off her red espadrilles and went swimming in the river in a voluminous black bathing dress. Sammy spent hours dangling a fishing line from the ancient bridge, earning himself the nickname 'Pettifish', while Belle's big eyes and short but shapely figure wreaked havoc with the artists who vied for her favours and came close to fighting a duel with pistols. Bob was utterly smitten, but the most witty and entertaining member of the company seemed incapable of expressing his love for her. Weary of Hyde-like 'two franc fucking', as he termed his functional visits to the Parisian '*maisons de tolérance*', he longed to experience a real romance like Louis's – but Belle had fallen for a young Irish artist called Frank O'Meira, and Bob's love for her was hopeless.

Meanwhile his sister in London was struggling to cope with two small children and a lack of housekeeping money. Had it not been for Henley's encouragement and commissions for reviews of books and art exhibitions, Katharine would have been in despair. Her cousin's attempts to keep track of what was happening to the money from her marriage settlement were being hampered by the inefficiency of the Edinburgh solicitor who was his fellow trustee, until an exasperated Louis complained to Bob: 'I can't get the Trust accounts from that egregious humbug Robert Robertson; I could kick his bum, if I could.'

Had Katharine been able to see across the English Channel to the enchanted glades of Fontainebleau, she might have envied her brother and cousin their carefree existence. Word had filtered back that Louis had found a new love in France, and in the autumn of 1877 he and Fanny paid a visit to London for her to have a small operation on an injured foot. This was the first opportunity to introduce her to his friends in England. What Katharine thought of the tough little American woman who had captured her cousin's heart is unrecorded, but to begin with Fanny found Louis's London friends charming and anxious to make her welcome.

De Mattos continued to treat his wife badly but Henley remained Katharine's rock in the storms of marital discord, offering her work – although Glasgow Brown could be tardy in paying her. 'The brutal and licentious Brown', as Louis now called him after falling out over Brown's handling of his Paris articles, had gone down with consumption and would soon be living out his last months in continental health resorts. This left the full burden of *London* on Henley's shoulders, but the rumbustious, one-legged buccaneer fought on manfully and did his best to sort out the financial mess left by Brown, informing Louis: 'I regret to say he's not paid Katharine (£5.2.6 for seven numbers), and I suppose he hasn't yet paid Ferrier either.'

Ferrier was now a published author, but the critics had not been kind to his novel which had failed to sell. Having left the Chambers Hospital, he remained in poor health, spending his days on the sofa as he struggled to write and to avoid thinking about the amber liquid that had become his

God. Drink had been what made life bearable, anaesthetising him to the real-isation that he would never achieve literary immortality like his illustrious ancestors, nor distinguish himself academically like his 'honoured father' or his brother-in-law Sir Alexander Grant, Principal of Edinburgh University. Ferrier's chief pleasure now, when he had the use of a carriage, was to be driven around what his friend Louis called the 'lamplit, vicious fairy land' of Edinburgh by night, waiting for the chemist's shops to appear – their gas-lit windows glowing with brightly coloured bottles whose contents might deaden pain and liberate the spirit from all care.

In early 1879, Henley got married to Anna Boyle, a plain but practical woman who had visited him in hospital in Edinburgh and remained close to him thereafter. Patient and undramatic, Anna was the perfect partner for her loudly outspoken, piratical husband who smoked like a chimney and drank copious quantities of whisky to deaden the pain of his leg as he entertained a circle of literary friends. The Henleys' London home in Shepherd's Bush would become a refuge for Katharine, who would always find a welcome there and a sympathetic ear.

Louis had not been at Henley's wedding but sent his best wishes from France. He had turned his canoe journey into his first book, An Inland Voy-age, and was now preparing it for publication. On his return in March he was able to give Henley his congratulations in person and see Katharine and Bob, who when not painting in France would stay with his mother in London where she had settled in Chelsea.

The critics had been cautiously kind to Louis's new book, but he was now writing in a different vein – a collection of comical short stories called New Arabian Nights, which Henley would serialise in *London*. The first three were about The Suicide Club, based on one of Bob's crazy ideas to which Louis and Katharine would be treated when he launched into his comic monologues. Louis used Bob as the model for the Young Man With The Cream Tarts, involved in a surreal stunt to rival their John Libbel esca-pades. The young man makes a tour of bars and cafes with a tray of tarts, offering them to customers – if they refuse, he must eat the tart himself. But behind the levity, the Young Man is weary of his existence and joins The Suicide Club, whose members draw playing cards to decide who will kill whom, thus freeing the grateful victim from life's cares.

At the Suicide Club, Louis created a sinister figure called Bartholomew Malthus: 'He was probably upwards of 40, but he looked fully ten years older; and Florizel thought he had never seen a man more naturally hideous, nor one more ravaged by disease and ruinous excitements. He was no more than skin and bone, was partly paralysed, and wore spectacles of such unusual power, that his eyes appeared through the glasses greatly magnified and distorted in shape.'

To any male Victorian reader, there was no mistaking the nature of the 'disease and ruinous excitements' leading to wasting muscles, deteriorating sight and paralysis, of which Louis had a lifelong horror. In dark, private moments he may have feared the appearance of the same symptoms, resulting from whatever ruinous excitements led to his health trip to Malvern with his mother. Yet bearing in mind that the Young Man was based on Bob, to whom New Arabian Nights would be dedicated, the black humour of the story would have personal resonances for him also – and for his sister.

Alan Stevenson's paralysis and mental deterioration had blighted their childhood until the dark cloud of doom was lifted by his death. Their feelings about their father may have been mixed, but Louis knew them well enough to know they would appreciate the next twist in the tale, as the Young Man draws the ace of clubs and is 'frozen with horror' to find he is to be the assassin. His victim, drawing the ace of spades, is the sinister paralytic. Shortly afterwards, a death is reported in the newspapers:

## *Melancholy Accident*

This morning, about two o'clock, Mr Bartholomew Malthus, of 16 Chepstow Place, Westbourne Grove, on his way home from a party at a friend's house, fell over the upper parapet in Trafalgar Square, fracturing his skull and breaking a leg and an arm. Death was instantaneous. Mr Malthus, accompanied by a friend, was engaged in looking for a cab at the time of the unfortunate occurrence. As Mr Malthus was paralytic, it is thought that his fall may have been occasioned by another seizure. The unhappy gentleman was well known in the most respectable circles, and his loss will be widely and deeply deplored.

As the unsuspected cause of death, pushing the paralytic over the parapet, how did Bob feel about this fictionalised act of patricide? Was it intended symbolically to liberate him and Katharine from their unhappy childhood? And how did she feel about Louis's choice of name for the victim? While it might be shared by the famous exponent of population growth theory, Malthus was also quite similar to Mattos – the paralysing blight on Katharine's life from which she longed to be liberated.

As Louis's stories appeared in Henley's *London*, he returned to France for some precious last weeks with Fanny Osbourne. Her husband had stopped sending money from California and for some time Louis had been supporting her and her family on his small literary earnings and allowance from his parents. Now Fanny had received an impatient telegram from San Francisco with the blunt message: 'Come home.' It seemed their grand Bohemian romance was over.

A passage to New York was booked for Fanny, Sammy and Belle – whose pleadings that she could not bear to be parted from O'Meira were not enough to persuade the Irishman to marry her. From one last, brief idyllic time together in Grez, Louis brought the Osbournes to London where Bob had found them lodgings in Radnor Street, Chelsea, just around the corner from his mother's home in St Leonard's Terrace. There they would stay for three weeks before catching the boat train to Liverpool.

To ease the unbearable sadness over losing the woman he loved, Louis threw himself into the life of a journalist, helping Henley with *London*. Young Sammy would recall how his childhood hero 'Luly' Stevenson seemed 'more mature and responsible. I was quite awed by his beautiful blue suit with its double-breasted coat, and the new stiff felt hat he threw on one side; and there was much in his eager talk about "going to press" and "closing the forms", and Henley "wanting a middle" about such and such a subject… He was constantly dashing up in cabs, and dashing away again with the impressive prodigality that apparently journalism required.'

On 12 August 1878, Louis saw Fanny, Belle and Sammy onto the train at Euston station. Sammy would recall: 'We were standing in front of our compartment, and the moment to say goodbye had come. It was terribly short and sudden and final, and before I could realise it RLS was walking away down the long length of the platform, a diminishing figure in a brown ulster. My eyes followed him, hoping that he would look back. But he never turned, and finally disappeared in the crowd.'

# 4

# The Runaway Wife

LOUIS DID NOT know if he would ever see Fanny Osbourne again. Unable to bear the thought of returning to Edinburgh, he set off for France, feeling 'pretty ill and pretty sad'. He needed a long walk with plenty of fresh air to clear his head. Louis was planning to write another travel book, this time a hike through the Cevennes Mountains in southern France with the novelty of a donkey for company. This took him to Le Monastier-sur-Gazeille, where he wrote to Henley: 'Here I am alone in this hill village, between nine and ten thousand metres above the sea.' As if to underline the point, he wrote to Charles Baxter as well: 'I am here alone in a hill village…'

Yet Louis was not alone. Some 46 years later, Katharine would reveal the secret which her cousin took great care not to disclose: 'He and I, with my baby daughter, travelled in France to many places. When he started on his journey "with a Donkey" we were there.' Katharine had packed a portmanteau of clothes for herself and three-year-old Snoodie and walked out on her husband, leaving her baby behind. And when Louis walked away from Euston station and booked his tickets for France, it seems he took his cousin and her little daughter with him – or met them shortly afterwards in Paris. For a young, single man to be travelling with a runaway wife was highly compromising, even if he were her cousin, and they may have decided to make separate journeys until they were out of the country.

At Le Monastier-sur Gazeille, Louis found lodgings with a family called Morel. He might be feeling desolate, but found life still had its compensations: 'The pension is three and a half francs, say three shillings a day; and the food capital, really good and plenteous, and the wine much stronger and pleasanter than most *ordinaires*. Besides which, there is some Saint Joseph, of which I sometimes treat myself to a bottle, which is gaudy fine stuff.'

There is no record of Katharine sharing the bottle, nor staying at the same pension. Even in Le Monastier-sur-Gazeille, whose peasant community of lace makers spoke plainly and swore like troopers, a young man sharing lodgings with a young lady and child who were clearly not his own might have caused tongues to wag. And while Louis may have been Katharine's protector as she took some breathing space to contemplate the wreck of her marriage, he needed solitude to write. Before setting off with a donkey, he had to complete his Arabian Nights stories for Henley and a collection of Picturesque Notes on Edinburgh, which Katharine may have been interested to take away and read while Snoodie had her afternoon nap.

The cousins shared an interest also in the darker side of Edinburgh's history – including the story of Deacon Brodie, which Louis and Henley were now turning into a play. William Brodie, born to a respectable life as a skilled cabinet maker and city councillor, had sought excitement in the drinking dens, cockfighting pits and dark closes of Edinburgh where he kept at least two secret mistresses who bore him children. For the ultimate thrill he led a gang of housebreakers, engaging in ever more audacious robberies until finally unmasked, apprehended and hanged before a crowd of respectable citizens, with some of whom he had spent pleasant evenings dining before returning at dead of night to rob them of their valuables.

Louis had been haunted by the spectre of Brodie since childhood, when a large wardrobe made by the Deacon's own hand had stood in a corner of his bedroom. Its looming presence there was the cause of many nightmares but also inspired one of his earliest attempts at story-writing, penned in the days of his apparent childhood romance with Katharine. The unfinished tale of Deacon Brodie had lain in the bottom of a trunk for years, until Henley got to hear about it – and suggested the two of them turn it into a play. The project became an obsession, at least on Henley's part, and Bob and Katharine were constantly informed of its progress. Even while buying a donkey and preparing for his mountain hike, Louis continued to fire off instructions about scenes and characters to his friend in London.

He set off on Sunday 22 September, around 6am with a bemused group of peasants looking on. Did Katharine and Snoodie rise early to wave off Louis and his new companion Modestine, or was she fanciful in stating that when he started on his journey with a donkey they were there? Certainly Katharine now faced the daunting prospect of surviving in France as a single mother, on a limited income, with an angry, deserted husband briefing lawyers back home, where a nursemaid had charge of the baby she had abandoned.

Meanwhile Louis pressed on with the journey that would be immortalised in his much-loved travel book, delighting readers with humorous accounts of his incompetent donkey-driving and damp nights huddled in a sleeping bag of sheepskin and tarpaulin, devouring an obscene meal of choc-olate and Bologna sausage washed down with neat brandy. At other times he lay under the stars, longing for the woman who was now so far away in California. There he feared Fanny might weaken and resign herself to life with Sam Osbourne, who had removed his latest floozy from the house in San Francisco before his family returned. If Osbourne could be persuaded to fornicate discretely elsewhere, might Fanny consent to patch things up and forget the love she had known in Grez? The little news Louis had from California was not good. On completing his journey he found three letters awaiting him from Fanny, 'for which I was glad and heartbroken'.

He now returned to London to stay with Henley and Anna in Shepherd's Bush, where the work on Deacon Brodie continued. Somehow Katharine held out in France, resisting the pressure to return to her husband and baby and live a lie in suburban servitude, struggling to pay the household bills while de Mattos pursued his Hyde-like pleasures elsewhere. But what was she holding out for? Did Katharine still harbour a secret hope that one day, despite all that had happened, she might somehow find happiness with the cousin she still loved more than anyone other than her brother Bob?

For now she remained a married woman, with a husband who took an intense interest in her whereabouts, as well as her money. It seems de Mat-tos got his solicitors to track her down, an intrusion resented by Louis who wrote to his lawyer friend Charles Baxter: 'The Lewises [for de Mattos] deny all knowledge of all the bad features of the case you know of; lay all blame on Gibson-Craig, Dalziel and Brodies [Katharine's solicitors in Edinburgh], and say it was bad conduct. Nice fellows you lawyers. The visit of the clerk to K. de M. they say is a malicious invention; such a thing, they say, could never happen in business. Nice fellows again.'

Louis had no wish to become entangled in a web of litigation which might lead to de Mattos suing him as Katharine's accomplice, or even nam-ing him as a correspondent. Anxious to avoid any visits by a lawyer's clerk serving a subpoena, he wrote from Henley's house to Baxter, 'I am still in France, please. Please remember that', and to his mother: 'Let no-one know I am here.'

Meanwhile Katharine was running out of money and had been forced to contact her husband, who refused to send her any. Instead de Mattos blamed her cousin, as one of her marriage settlement trustees, for leaving her short of cash. Unable to contact Louis directly, he sent a terse telegram to Charles

Baxter: 'Lewis [sic] grossly careless. Send £10 to Katharine D.M. to poste restante Paris to avoid subpoena. Will write you.'

Baxter complied at once before informing Louis, who responded: 'I had already sent money to France; but in the matter of money, the more the merrier.' He found the behaviour of de Mattos contemptible: 'Our man makes about as much as I do, has more to do with this complication, and has no heavier load upon his shoulders. If it would do anything else but bring trouble on his wife, I should write myself and advertise him of my views. As it is, if you have a *natural* means of commenting on his conduct in a business way, I should not mind you hinting that his action was a little more than cool, and his language a thought less than – well, let us say – considerate. At any rate, honour no more telegrams from him... On the other hand, should Katharine (separately) ask an advance, do not hesitate to honour it.'

Money worries aside, Katharine in Paris was beginning to fret about the baby she had left behind. Richard was nominally with his father, then living next door to Katharine's mother in Chelsea. In the circumstances, the tension between the two households might easily be imagined. Yet curiously Louis had been unable to envisage the strength of his cousin's maternal feelings after three months away from her baby. She was desperate to get Richard back. Eventually, Louis informed Baxter: 'I have found out what was the matter with Katharine; it was her kid, about which, honestly I had forgot.'

De Mattos might be glad to rid himself of a child of 19 months, but was determined not to appear complicit in Katharine's decision to leave him. For the sake of appearances, and the lawyers, it was important for him to be seen as a kind and responsible husband who had sent his wife away to France for the good of her health, not a callous, fornicating brute whose cruelty had driven her to run away in despair. To get Richard safely back with his mother in France, Louis outlined a plan to Baxter: 'The kid, if you report favourably of our position, shall be forwarded afterwards. I propose the husband to say:

(1) That he had met Katharine in town, thought her looking ill and packed her to the country.
(2) After a few days, that he believed she couldn't stand this excitement and had packed her abroad.

Then, as it seems to me, he could send the child after; and, sticking to the same story, refuse her address. This system I shall develop to the husband tonight; should you not think it good or safe, or should your studies convince you we are dealing with a more ticklish state of affairs, please advise him to that effect. W Sydney de Mattos, 17 St Leonard's Terrace, Chelsea.'

As 1878 drew to a close, Louis returned to Edinburgh in time for Christmas and the constant round of social callers at the Stevensons' home in Heriot Row, where his parents were delighted to introduce him as the author of Edinburgh Picturesque Notes. His heart might lie 5000 miles away in San Francisco, from which came little hope, but for a while he was happy to be back in the city he both loved and hated in equal measure. Baxter and Gracie were glad to see him and introduce him to their new son Edmund at their home in Rutland Square. Witnessing this picture of domestic bliss, in contrast to his own troubled love life, Louis could not help feeling a pang of envy.

But others also did not have their sorrows to seek. Walter Ferrier, whose poor, paralysed mother had died that summer, had again gone off the rails. After the failure of his novel, he had made half-hearted attempts to get Blackwood to commission more work from him, and had been offered the chance to write leading articles for *The Scotsman* newspaper, but confessed: 'I am totally unable to write anything – least of all a *Scotsman* leader. O ye gods! I have a most unaccountable stricture (mental) and cannot get anything said. Perhaps I've nothing to say!' In a letter to Henley he admitted to 'having many *mauvais quarts d'heure*' for which the only remedy seemed to be the bottle. That Christmas and New Year found Ferrier frequently too full of the festive spirit, transformed by his addiction into a slobbering, stumbling brute.

Yet behind the bloated mask of Mr Hyde the alcoholic, Louis could still discern the kindly, witty, courteous young man of whom he had once been in awe. The war in the members between Ferrier drunk and sober did damage only to poor Walter himself, and perhaps his sister Coggie who still strove to return him to the straight and narrow. In others with a split personality the conflict could be far more sinister. As Louis went out to Swanston Cottage that January to spend a week with Henley, working on the double life of Deacon Brodie, he must have been reminded of another dark character whose life ended on the gallows. During Louis's last stay at Swanston, eight months previously, he had gone into Edinburgh to see Eugene Chantrelle tried for murder.

While Brodie had led two separate lives, he was essentially the same person – but Chantrelle was a full-blown, Jekyll and Hyde psychopath. Outwardly mild-mannered, he supported his young wife and family by working as a French tutor. He was one of three French speakers with whom Louis liked to spend the occasional hour in an Edinburgh public house. But while Victor Richon was a decent fellow and Henri van Laun, for all his drunken bluster, was essentially harmless, Chantrelle was a violent alcoholic with an undisclosed criminal history of rape and murder.

He had come to Scotland after serving a nine-month prison sentence in England for a grossly indecent assault on a girl pupil at the school where he worked. Settling in Edinburgh, he advertised for a housekeeper and on New Year's Day, 1867, Lucy Holme came for an interview. Seeking escape from an unhappy life with her clergyman father and an unkind stepmother, she wanted only to be able to support herself financially – and found herself alone in the house with the brooding Frenchman. After satisfying himself as to her suitability for the post and offering her a glass of claret, which she refused, Chantrelle casually pushed her to the floor, pulled up her skirt and petticoats, tore open her bloomers and raped her.

Miss Holme, as innocent and ignorant as Katharine on her wedding day, had no idea of the consequences until months later. In desperation, she then wrote to the man who had ruined her: 'You cannot be surprised when I tell you that I expect to be confined in *three* months time, and *you*, and *you only*, are the *father* of the child, and if I should not get over it, you too will be responsible for my death. I have left my situation, as governess, for my holidays, but in the state I find myself I cannot possibly return. Something *must* be done, and you are the only one to do it...'

Deaf to her entreaties, Chantrelle did nothing and left her to the shame of bringing up her child alone. By now he had other worries, having got a 16-year-old pupil pregnant at Newington Academy. This time he could not avoid his responsibilities and had to marry Elizabeth Dyer, whose bump was clearly visible through the crinolines on their wedding day. For her, marriage would mean a decade of misery, living with a man who was perfectly affable by day and in public, but who forced himself upon her at night or left the house in a drunken rage for the brothels of Clyde Street, where he carried a revolver and occasionally shot holes in the windows, to the terror of the girls and their customers.

In the end, having insured his wife's life for a large sum, Chantrelle gave her a fatal dose of opium and claimed she had been poisoned by a gas leak. It took the detective skills of the Edinburgh medical professor Joseph Bell, on whom Conan Doyle based Sherlock Holmes, to expose Chantrelle's ruse and secure a conviction for murder. Louis, as a qualified advocate watching the trial, was told by the prosecution that a string of previous murders involving opium might be laid at the Frenchman's door. But one was enough for justice to prevail and on 31 May, after a breakfast of eggs and coffee but denied his last request of 'three bottles of champagne and a whore', Chantrelle was led into the execution shed at the Calton Jail and dispatched with an eight-foot drop by the hangman.

Louis, stunned to discover the depths of depravity that had lurked within his former drinking crony, was left to reflect: 'I should say, looking back from the unfair superior ground of subsequent knowledge, that Chantrelle bore upon his brow the most open marks of criminality; or rather, I should say so if I had not met another man who was his exact counterpart in looks, and who was yet, by all that I could learn of him, a model of kindness and good conduct.' He now had more than enough material to create Mr Hyde.

After completing Deacon Brodie, Louis went down to London where he and Henley were keen to interest Sir Henry Irving in staging the play and perhaps taking the role of the Deacon himself. The great actor manager was less keen, as Louis confessed in a letter home to his mother: 'Continued chase of the wild Henry Irving. He flees before me like the night. He is silent as the Sphynx; but I persevere...'

Yet for all the play's dark and dramatic content, it was never going to be an attractive commercial proposition. Louis turned his attention to reading the proofs of *Travels with a Donkey in the Cevennes*, with the help of Ferrier. For light relief, they would pen the odd *blague* or spoof letter to Bob, now staying at his mother's home in Chelsea. There the family crisis over Katharine's desertion of de Mattos had developed new complications. Her sister Mab's marriage to Alec Gibson Thomson, son of a wealthy wine merchant, seemed to be heading likewise for the rocks – and Gibson Thomson blamed Katharine for encouraging Mab to end it. Bob refrained from apportioning blame but, after an unpleasant encounter with his sister's husband, told Louis: 'I don't care about seeing much of him for I don't understand him or what part he had in the affair.'

Gibson Thomson's bad-mouthing of his sister-in-law had already reached her cousin, who replied: 'As for Alec I have nothing to do with him, if I do not hit him in the mouth. I am not certain which. He behaved so piggish about Katharine; everybody is against K. and swallows his scandal and filth about her like milk, that I mean to show I won't. It's not anger or revenge, all which soon falls from me; it's loyalty to Katharine. Damn me if he ever shakes my hand, in any other spirit but that of hostility.'

Mab would eventually divorce the unlovely Alec and later that year would marry George Chardin Denton, a former soldier now entering the colonial service as Chief of Police on the Caribbean island of St Vincent, who would rise to be Governor of Gambia. Meanwhile Louis still clung to the hope of finding happiness with Fanny Osbourne, who he learned was now living in Monterey apart from her husband in San Francisco.

Not knowing what the outcome would be, Louis poured his feelings into writing The Story of a Lie, about Dick Naseby's love for Esther van Tromp. Dick, who like Louis has been leading a Bohemian life with a group of artists in Paris, returns to his father's house in the Vale of Thyme, easily recognisable as the surroundings of Swanston Cottage at the foot of the Pentland Hills. There Dick chances upon Esther, sitting on a rock sketching. She is wearing a black dress, as Fanny was when Louis first met her, and shares her first name with Esther Vandegrift, Fanny's mother.

But in describing the start of their love affair, Louis may also have evoked memories of a childhood romance which Katharine would have read with mixed feelings, recalling how they had once lain together under the trees, reading the adventures of Dick Turpin. Now there was a new love in the scenario, walking hand in hand with Dick Naseby: 'The path they were following led them through a wood of pine trees carpeted with heather and blueberry, and upon this pleasant carpet Dick, not without some seriousness, made her sit down.

'Esther!' he began, 'There is something you ought to know. You know my father is a rich man, and you would think, now that we love each other, we might marry when we pleased. But I fear, darling, we may have long to wait and shall want all our courage.'

In the story, the obstacles to Dick and Esther's happiness are their fathers – Esther's drunken and disreputable, Dick's respectable and censorious. In real life the obstacles were Fanny's disreputable husband, and Louis's God-fearing father who would be horrified at the thought of him taking another man's wife and could not accept his son's intentions were honourable. Dick's cry from the heart to Esther is not fiction but autobiography: 'You do not understand; you do not know what it is to be treated with daily want of comprehension and daily small injustices, through childhood and boyhood and manhood, until you despair of a hearing, until the thing rides you like a nightmare, until you almost hate the sight of the man you love, and who's your father after all... My father is the best man I know in all this world; he is worth a hundred of me, only he doesn't understand me, and he can't be made to.'

Esther's solution is that they should elope, but Dick is perplexed by her apparent coldness towards him as she repeats, without emotion: 'I want you to take me away.' Did Fanny really love Louis, or did she just see him as a way out of her loveless marriage? Louis's own anxiety and insecurity is evident in the story as Dick pleads with Esther: 'You know well who I am, and what I am, and that I love you. You say I will not help you; but your heart knows the contrary. It is you who will not help me; for you will not tell me what you want...'

As Louis wrote the story, he was tormented by the thought that Fanny did not love him and might resign herself to living a lie with her faithless husband. Her letters were infrequent and did not always make sense, causing him to fear she might be suffering a breakdown. Even in the happy surroundings of Grez she had sometimes shown signs of mental instability. Now Louis, knowing he might be summoned at any moment, was trying to save up £400 for a trip to America. This meant visits to London were on a shoestring, and to save money he arranged to stay with Aunt Alan in Chelsea.

This plunged him into the final throes of Mab's marital difficulties with Gibson Thomson. Anxious not to upset her mother, Mab had confided in her Aunt Maggie in Edinburgh. Louis's mother had passed on the letter to apprise him of the situation, which became more complicated when Gibson Thomson sought a reconciliation. 'G.T. has written and all is to be made right,' Louis wrote home. 'Under these circumstances I thought I did right to suppress Mab's letter to you, which could only have given pain to Aunt Alan. Was I not right? I keep it in case you think otherwise...'

With the summer Bob returned to France, but not to Grez. He was now painting in the little town of Cernay-la-Ville, where Louis joined him and they were able to share memories of happier times. The land of Bohemia seemed strange without the Osbournes, and Louis's hopes of rejoining them were full of uncertainty. Fanny was finding it hard to cope with only grudging financial support from her husband, and Louis was now sending her money via her brother – but still she showed no sign of wanting him by her side. He returned from France to London and, receiving no news there, went back up to Scotland to wait.

The telegram from California came as his parents were preparing for a health trip to a spa resort in Cumberland. They were expecting Louis to accompany them, but he met them at the station to say he had been called away on 'business'. With the coast clear, he swiftly made arrangements for a transatlantic crossing on the SS Devonia, sailing from the Clyde. He then made a quick trip to London to say goodbye to Henley and his other friends, all of whom had misgivings. Bob, who might have pursued his cousin to bring him back, was kept in the dark along with Katharine and Aunt Alan. Baxter, who had been briefed on Louis's plans throughout, was out of town but told his friend he could stay at his empty house in Edinburgh before setting off on the voyage.

This left Louis to break the news to poor, alcoholic Walter Ferrier who had relied on his friendship to get him through that year. On the night before Louis was due to sail, Ferrier showed up drunk on the doorstep of Baxter's house in Rutland Square, greatly distressed to learn his friend was leaving for an uncertain future and they might never meet again. Louis would be haunted by the memory: 'I waited hours for him, and at last he came. "My God," I said, "You have had too much again." He did not deny it, as he did in the old days. He said, "Yes," with a terrible simplicity... This fresh humiliation, after all the brave words and projects, accepted so plainly and so humbly, it went to my heart like a knife... We sat late, in Baxter's empty house where I was sleeping, and when we parted, for the only time, we parted with a kiss.'

# 5

# A Married Man

IN 1880 LOUIS Stevenson returned from America with a wife. The new Mrs Stevenson, short, stocky and with dark, flashing eyes, was a woman of 40 with greying hair who worried that she might not live up to the rather flattering photograph of herself which she had sent Louis's parents. But her new mother-in-law was quick to reassure her she was 'just like her photo' and to welcome her into the family along with 12-year-old Sam, 'very fair with no colour in his face at all' and still bearing the name of the father he had left behind in California.

From now on Fanny would have a full-time job as her husband's ever-vigilant nurse. The disease that had lain dormant in Louis for years had risen to the surface during his voyage on the emigrant ship and turned his long train journey across the plains to San Francisco into a fevered nightmare. By the time he reached Monterey his health was broken, and the physical wreck who appeared on Fanny's doorstep hardly seemed a viable alternative to the man he was hoping she would divorce.

This had been a long process, with Louis living in cheap lodgings in Monterey while Fanny went back to the little wooden house in Oakland which had been her dowry and which her husband had now vacated. Sam Osbourne had a respectable position to maintain at the law courts and took care to keep his affairs discreet, but the scandal of a very public divorce might make life difficult. He did not want all San Francisco knowing his wife was leaving him for another man because he could not keep his hands off other women. Any divorce had to be done quietly on his terms, with a respectable interval until Fanny remarried, if she wanted to keep custody of young Sam.

So Louis stayed in Monterey for a while, struggling to write and plagued by ill health that seemed to attack his chest. At last the divorce came through and he was able to move to cheap lodgings in San Francisco, still staying away from Oakland where Fanny lived respectably with her sister Nellie. Louis would see her twice a week in a cheap restaurant, and every time she saw him he seemed thinner and more flushed in the face, his eyes burning feverishly and his emaciated body racked by a persistent cough. Eventually she insisted he move to a hotel in Oakland where she could keep an eye on him, and by good fortune was there when the first haemorrhage came. Struggling to calm him as the blood gushed from his mouth, she cried out for a doctor. He managed to stem the flow – but then pronounced Louis a hopeless case of galloping consumption, unlikely to last more than a few weeks.

Yet Louis had not died, and nobody close to him would ever become consumptive, although he would spend the next decade in the shadow of the life-threatening affliction he called 'bluidy jack'. With his future now uncertain, he wanted to marry Fanny as soon as possible, so she could at least claim a widow's pension as the wife of an Edinburgh advocate. Ignoring propriety, they married in San Francisco five months after the divorce. Then the 'very withered bridegroom' was taken off to convalesce in the clean, Californian mountain air, camping out at a deserted silver mine where Fanny's skills as a frontierswoman turned a derelict, windowless bunkhouse into the makeshift sanatorium immortalised in *The Silverado Squatters*.

By now Louis had been reconciled with his parents. On first discovering their son had gone to America on what his father called 'this sinful mad business', the Stevensons had been distraught, and even considered leaving Edinburgh where they could no longer hold up their heads in society. But as the months passed and their son's life-threatening illness put respectability into perspective, Louis was forgiven and Tom Stevenson booked first-class cabins to bring his son home with his new family. Soon Fanny and young Sam were made to feel at home in Heriot Row, where Mrs Stevenson insisted on giving her daughter-in-law the run of her wardrobe while Louis's father was quite taken with the feisty little American woman who teased him and called him 'Master Tommy'.

This picture of unconventional married bliss was in sharp contrast to Katharine's plight in London. The shock of Louis's sudden departure to America, followed by news of his marriage, had finally put paid to any secret hope of one day finding happiness as his wife. Under intense social pressure and moral outrage stoked by the likes of Alec Gibson Thomson, she had given in and gone back to her unfaithful husband. With the two children, they had moved away from her mother in Chelsea to a house in Kensington. De Mattos continued to give private tuition in mathematics, making a living in the same way as Eugene Chantrelle with his French lessons, although fortunately not with the same consequences. Katharine thought it best not to ask where her husband was going when he left the house as she was putting the children to bed.

To help pay the bills, they took in lodgers. Servants were cheap, so they employed three girls in their 20s. With Emily Harris, Mary Blogg and Amy Rogers living under the same roof as de Mattos, Katharine would do well to keep a close eye on her husband. Meanwhile, she remained determined to support herself through writing. Louis might have abandoned her as a mentor but Henley remained a staunch friend. Since the demise of the short-lived *London*, he had been struggling to make a living himself but had found work with publications such as the *Saturday Review* and may have helped Katharine get a toehold there.

In the autumn of 1880, Louis, Fanny and Sam came south. They had spent what passed for a Scottish summer in the Highlands with Louis's parents, during which it became clear that winter north of the Border could prove a death sentence for the invalid author. His uncle Dr George Balfour recommended wintering in Switzerland and the Louis Stevensons were now on their way to the health resort of Davos. Before leaving Scotland they wrote a joint letter to Bob, with Fanny telling him: 'I can hardly believe that I am going back to London again, or that I am to see you and Katharine once more. I long to see Katharine. I have always thought her one of the finest creatures going, though I should have liked her all the same if she were not. There are some people that one likes naturally, and to me Katharine is one of those. The reverse case I fear is not true; it very seldom is...'

Was this just Fanny's insecurity, or did she know of her husband's childhood romance with his cousin and sense a lingering resentment on Katharine's part? Rather than visit her at the unhappy house in Kensington, Fanny and Louis invited Katharine, Bob and her mother to see them at the Grosvenor Hotel where they kept open house to friends. In a letter to his parents, Louis reported: 'Aunt Alan fat; Bob better; Katharine looking, I think, a little haggard.'

She was presented with a tail-less cat which Fanny had been given as a wedding present – 'Manxy is intrusted to Katharine' – before the invalid author and his nurse departed for Davos. They would not risk a return to Scotland until the following May. By then they had expended large sums and Charles Baxter, who had charge of Louis's finances, was exasperated. Henley urged patience, warning him he would 'have to deal with a sick child, who is the husband of a schoolgirl of forty'. Fanny's volatile temperament, with violent likes and dislikes bordering sometimes on paranoia, had led him to christen her 'the Bedlamite'. Yet the one-legged man, perhaps trying to over-come his own resentment of the woman responsible for the change in his friend, also entreated Baxter: 'Be as kind and as nice to Mrs Louis as ever you can. I have seen much of her, and I have modified a good deal. I like her some, and I can't help pitying her much.'

Louis, Fanny and Sam returned from Switzerland to Scotland to spend the summer of 1881 in the Highlands with his parents, taking shelter from the traditional deluge in a cottage in Braemar. Such was the fear of haemor-rhages that Louis had to keep to his bed and was not allowed to speak until the afternoon. The conditions were ripe for *Treasure Island*.

It began with a map, drawn to keep young Sam amused, although the person most excited by the story that developed was Tom Stevenson, who enthusiastically enumerated the contents of Billy Bones' chest. Yet the central character who came to dominate the tale was inspired by a burly, bearded, swashbuckling figure now casting around for a new berth as an editor 500 miles away. In Louis's imagination, William Ernest Henley became Long John Silver, a charismatic figure despite all his backstabbing treachery.

The story advanced at a chapter a day, read out by Louis to the family each night, and arrangements were made for serialisation in Young Folks magazine. But by the 18th chapter the author had dried up, shortly after Silver had struck the murderous First Blow, burying his knife in poor Tom's defenceless body as the dying Alan's scream rose from the distant marsh. Was Mr Stevenson amused to be the victim of this symbolic act of patricide, along with Bob and Katharine's poor father? Writer's block descended and Louis, wearing a 'pig's snout' respirator after his lungs took a turn for the worse, was soon under doctor's orders to return to Switzerland.

He, Fanny and Sam were to break their journey in London, where Louis told Henley they would be staying in Chelsea with Aunt Alan at 'St Leon-ard's terrace, six and ten, where lives or lived the prince of men, Bobus...' The prince of men, already realising that his dream of becoming a great artist would never become reality, had been plunged into deep, hopeless melancholy by the news that Belle Osbourne had got married in California. After her speedy recovery from her love affair with Frank O'Meara, Bob had dared to hope he was in with a chance and had written to her – only to learn Fanny's daughter had already wed another artist, Joe Strong.

Bleakly Katharine's brother now had to accept Belle would never be his. Still struggling to paint in France, he had written to Louis in Monterey: 'Never mind my letters to Belle, it is of no consequence now... No, Belle is married. I hope she will be happy. I think she is a person to get to like a man she is with. I cannot think or look forward to being any cause of future disagreement, besides, I have accustomed myself to regard the world as a place not to be happy in, or as not intended for a moment for that purpose... Art is occasionally an amusement but I only care for it when it is about the future life, so now in painting I only care for vast, empty, *triste* landscapes with something somewhere in the sky that looks like hope and mystery – I can't do it because I can't paint, but thinking about it is some pleasure.'

Bob's 'Paris girl', the blonde Portuguese model who had shared his bed in Paris, was going away to Brazil, leaving him with feelings of regret that he had never given her the love she deserved. The one glimmer of hope in his life was Louisa Purland, the pretty daughter of a London dentist. She supported herself through freelance journalism and seemed keen to rescue Bob from the dark direction his thoughts were taking. He told Louis: 'I have just got a letter from her begging me to let her send me coin and asking me to come to London, as she thinks I am out of it here, and will get into a bad frame of mind... She is very unhappy herself, also, but then she has more life and force than I have. I will not take the coin, not that I mind, only I won't. She has made 64 quid by literature since I have been here, two or three months. Misfortunes make her work. It is very curious. How can she care?'

Secretly, because Louisa's father disapproved of him, Bob and Louisa got married in London, but initially continued to live apart. Together they would make the best they could of life, even if they saw each other only occasionally. Louis described her as 'a sensible young woman, with lots of pluck and activity – a contrast to Bob'. Eight months later, when their marriage became public, Louis wrote to his mother: 'I am glad Bob has told you. The idea was not to tell until he could support her. When will that be?' Aunt Alan, on learning her son was married, had been filled with anxiety: 'Her heart was in her boots, she did not know what kind of creature a madman like Bob would bring home... and when the door opened she was overjoyed.'

For Katharine, who idolised the brother who confided in her, it must have been hard to share him with another woman, especially when her own marriage was such a failure. De Mattos did not seem happy to have her back and continued to mistreat his unhappy wife. Louis could see this only too clearly when he met Katharine in Chelsea, and was now encouraging her to leave her husband forever. Divorce was a difficult, expensive and scandalous option, but a legal separation might keep de Mattos's hands off Katharine's money and ensure she had custody of the children.

Yet even now Katharine hesitated, reluctant to accept that Snoodie and Richard's father would never be any good. Louis had enlisted the help of his lawyer friend Baxter and wrote to him from Davos: 'I cannot say how much obliged I am to you for this kindness about K. de M. A firm hand is needed to keep her to it; but I believe a good solicitor would do the trick.' With this Louis included a formal request 'to inspect on my behalf the Marriage Contract of Mr and Mrs Sydney de Mattos and the securities of the investments'.

As Baxter put the wheels in motion to end Katharine's unhappy marriage, she felt the full force of disapproval from de Mattos's friends and family. To leave a husband, no matter how abusive or unfaithful, was a scandalous thing. To right-minded Victorians, her wilful behaviour in finding herself a job and taking her children away from their father was quite deplorable. Yet amid all the opprobrium heaped upon her, a letter from Louis brought a smile to Katharine's face as he made of joke of the heavy moral outrage: 'I hope you know that we both loathe, deprecate, detest and sicken at the thought of you. Never lose sight of that. Again assuring you of my uncontrollable disgust, Believe me, Yours abhorrently...'

Louis had turned his attention to *Treasure Island* once more. In the crisp, clear mountain air of Davos, the tale began to flow freely again, dispelling fears that the serial now running in Young Folks magazine might suffer an embarrassing breakdown. Unlike Louis's highly stylised novel *Prince Otto*, whose obscure plot failed to capture the imagination despite years of polishing and repolishing, *Treasure Island* had a life of its own, vivid and true on every page.

Meanwhile the vivid inspiration for Long John Silver had boarded a new vessel and seized the helm. Since the collapse of *London*, the burly, one-legged Henley had been in the doldrums, placing articles where he could, but at last he had secured another editorship. Under his swashbuckling command, the *Magazine of Art* would prosper as one of Cassell & Co's most influential publications, full of innovative writing by gifted new authors such as RL Stevenson. Henley was not only eager to commission articles from his friend but never missed an opportunity to promote his work and keep Louis's name in the public eye.

He was also acting as his literary agent without pay, always mindful of the help Louis had given him when he was on his beam ends in the Edinburgh infirmary. Henley's negotiating style with publishers was fearless. In the spring of 1883, he walked into an editor's office at Cassell with a bundle of magazine proofs and slammed them down on the desk, declaring: 'There's a book for ye!' *Treasure Island* had done moderately well as a Young Folks serial but was about to emerge from the smoke and fire of Henley's negotiations as an international bestseller. Cassell capitulated to his demand for an advance of five times what Louis had been paid for his first travel book – leaving the author beside himself with joy.

'Dear child,' he wrote to Henley, on hearing the offer. 'O golden voice, enchanting warbler of the evening glade, sun of the ardent tropic, angel friend: One Hundred Pounds (and to a beggar) TAKE, O TAKE, IT! LET IT WAVE!'

His money worries were over, with enough to pay his rent for six months in advance. Louis, Fanny and Sam were now living in a little house called La Solitude in Hyères near Toulon. Louis's delicate health could no longer stand the Scottish climate, and he could not face the prospect of permanent incarceration in the frozen Alps, so the South of France seemed his best bet. There life was good, strolling in the large garden of a summer's evening to the sound of nightingales in the woods.

From England came good news from Bob and Louisa, who were now the parents of a little girl, diplomatically christened Margaret after her paternal grandmother, although everyone in the family called her Pootle. It seemed strange but pleasant to Louis to imagine Bob 'smiling on his kid' back in England. Meanwhile there was the excitement of drawing up a suitable map for *Treasure Island*, which was taking a long time to come to birth – the first 2,000 copies would not emerge from the presses until the middle of November.

Five weeks before that, bad news from London took the wind out of Louis's sails. On September 9, Walter Ferrier lost his battle with the demon alcohol and died of chronic Bright's disease at the lodgings where he had spent his last months near Henley in Shepherd's Bush. Poor Ferrier's inner Hyde had triumphed over the once-beautiful and talented young man, and his friend was devastated by the news: 'My poor, besotted gentleman. O what regrets, what regrets! I wish to God I could have gone to his funeral even. Christ pity us: the hearse to take him away, that old fount of laughter…'

For weeks Louis could write of little other than Ferrier's death, until Fanny began to fear for his health. Racked with guilt for not doing more to help his friend, Louis sought consolation in writing to Ferrier's sister Coggie. Pouring out his heart, he assured her that her brother, 'set apart that terrible disease, was, in his right mind, the best and kindest gentleman. God knows he would never intentionally hurt a soul. Well, he is done with his troubles and out of his long sickness, and I dare say is glad to be at peace and out of the body, which in him seemed the enemy of the fine and kind spirit.' Brooding over the Jekyll and Hyde personalities at war for so long within his unfortunate friend, Louis reflected that in death 'the good, true Ferrier obliterates the memory of the other, who was only his 'lunatic brother'. The sense of loss, so strong that one evening Louis could have sworn Ferrier was in the room with him and heard 'his rich laughter', made him acutely aware of how much he valued his friends. He wrote to Katharine: 'The horrid jog of my poor Ferrier's departure has brought all my affections more clearly to my eyes.'

Louis had been penning 'penny whistles' or rhymes for children that would eventually become *A Child's Garden of Verses*, and asked his cousin to try some of them out on Snoodie. Much though Katharine might appreciate these expressions of affection, as a single mother struggling to bring up two children on an uncertain income from freelance journalism she must have found it hard to learn her cousin's burgeoning talents as a writer had brought him £330 that year – of which more than a third would go on Sam's school fees.

Yet Louis worked hard for his money, and had just reached the end of a serialisation marathon in *Young Folks* magazine, churning out chapters of *The Black Arrow* so furiously that he literally lost the plot and had to be reminded by the proof reader that he had reached the final chapter without killing off the villainous Sir Daniel Brackley. Katharine, who read everything her favourite cousin wrote with interest, may have bought copies of Young Folks to follow the dashing exploits of Louis's young hero – again called Dick, but this time with the surname Shelton. As Dick rode to the rescue of the lovely Joanna Sedley, did Katharine catch an echo of her own childhood adventures with the author?

At the end of 1883, Louis sent Katharine a postal order for 20 francs or around £1 as a New Year present. Under heavy prompting from Henley, he offered belated compliments on her paper for the *Magazine of Art* on Flowers and Flower-Painters, published three months earlier: 'I wondered how you had managed to make such an advance.' And he assured his cousin: 'My dearest Katharine, you must never think that silence is anything more than selfishness on our part. For I believe my wife loves and admires you, and know that I do from my heart.'

At the start of 1884, Louis could share memories of Ferrier with Henley and Baxter when they came for a visit. Together they had once imagined each other as the Four Musketeers – Ferrier as Athos, Henley as Porthos, Baxter as Aramis and Louis the quick-tempered D'Artagnan. Now one of them lay in the grave, commemorated by Henley in a poem: 'Our Athos rests – the wise, the kind, the liberal and august, his fault atoned...'

To escape such maudlin sentiments, the surviving musketeers took a trip to Monaco, Monte Carlo and Menton, returning via Nice. There Henley and Baxter boarded the train home, while Louis and Fanny stayed on for a few days. In the hotel he became so seriously ill that Fanny feared he might die and wired Henley back in London, who immediately sent out Bob on a rescue mission. Together Bob and Fanny got the invalid back to Hyères, but it had been touch and go.

Bob returned to London, where he could reassure Henley, Katharine and his mother that Louis was on the mend. Then in April, Coggie Ferrier paid a long-promised visit to Hyères. Ferrier's sister was friendly with Katharine in London and had been writing to Louis since he sent her a letter of condolence. There must have been tears on their first meeting at La Solitude, but Coggie was a strong character with all the wit and vivacity her poor mother had possessed before the paralysis set in. She also had her own talent for mimicry which Louis loved, declaring: 'Coggie Ferrier has kept us in steady laughter since her coming; she is as good as a regiment; huge fun; and she and Fanny get along nicely.'

Already *Treasure Island* was into its second edition and Louis's fame was growing, but suddenly it seemed he might not survive to enjoy celebrity. Coggie was still staying with the Stevensons when something in his chest gave way and the two women found themselves fighting to save his life. Fanny would recall how 'the blood spurted all over everything in a moment. He was almost strangled with it... I caught nearly a pint of blood in a basin besides what went on towels and things'. Three hours later, Louis 'awoke and poured, literally poured, forth another volume of blood equal in quantity to the first. He is very weak and getting light headed.'

Even when the bleeding stopped, the local doctor seemed to think Louis would not live for long, and Fanny wrote in desperation to London: 'If it is not the end, Henley, it is the beginning of the end...' Henley at once secured the services of Dr Zebulon Mennell, who set off for the South of France, his fee guaranteed by the two remaining musketeers and Bob, out of their own pockets. Mennell found Louis seriously ill but not a hopeless case, so long as he followed good medical advice. Fanny was now convinced this could be found only in England, and that their idyllic life in Hyères must end. It was time to abandon the South of France for the South of England – and a villa in the seaside town of Bournemouth.

# 6

# Birth of a Monster

FOR THE FIRST time Louis was now a householder, although the villa had been purchased by Tom Stevenson for Fanny as the more responsible adult. Louis christened it Skerryvore, after the great Stevenson lighthouse built by Bob and Katharine's father, a miniature version of which soon graced the garden. From London, Bournemouth was readily accessible by train and friends could come on visits. When Louis and Fanny moved into their new home in April 1885, Katharine gave them a pair of Japanese vases as a housewarming present, and for the next two years she would be a frequent, much-loved house guest.

With Henley's help, Katharine was becoming established as an art critic and woman of taste, and Fanny continued to profess the greatest admiration for her husband's favourite female cousin. Louis now was able to introduce Katharine to his growing circle of literary admirers, including Sir Percy Shelley. As a devotee of horror stories, Katharine may have been disappointed to discover that the son of the romantic poet and the creator of Frankenstein's monster was not in the least bit scary but an amiable, eccentric country squire who lived with his wife at Boscombe Manor on the outskirts of Bournemouth.

Henry James, the American novelist, called on the Stevensons and ended up visiting every night during his ten-week stay in the town. But while James became a firm friend, there were some admirers Louis did not cultivate – notably Prime Minister William Gladstone, who had been so enthralled by *Treasure Island* that he sat up all night reading it. Louis, who blamed Gladstone for the national disgrace of the fall of Khartoum with the death of General Gordon, was unimpressed, telling his mother: 'It appears Gladstone talks all the time about *Treasure Island*; he would do better to attend to the imperial affairs of England.'

In a different vein, Louis had been working on a second collection of new *Arabian Nights* stories, this time with the help of Fanny who had contributed two of them, duly polished up by Louis to the same standard as the rest. The stories appeared as *The Dynamiter*, with Fanny's name on the cover as co-author. Katharine, trying unsuccessfully to get her own short stories published, might be forgiven a pang of envy on seeing how easy it was for the wife of a popular author to appear in print. But whenever Katharine came on a visit to Skerryvore, she could at least bathe in some of the *Treasure Island* author's reflected glory and meet some of her cousin's new literary friends.

She was staying in Bournemouth in August 1885 when Louis decided they should all go on a jaunt to see Thomas Hardy at Max Gate, the popular West Country author's big new house outside Dorchester, built on the proceeds of *Under the Greenwood Tree*, *Far From the Madding Crowd* and *The Return of the Native*. Rather than impose too far on Hardy's hospitality, the Stevensons stayed nearby at the King's Arms Hotel. The visit itself was uneventful, with Fanny finding Hardy a 'pale, gentle, frightened little man, that one felt an instinctive tenderness for', but there was more than enough drama when the Stevensons went on to Exeter. There, at the New London Hotel, Louis took a massive haemorrhage.

Suddenly the hotel bedroom became a scene of a bloody horror as the two women fought to save his life. In a letter to Henley, Fanny would confide: 'Fortunately Katharine was with us, and was of the utmost use and comfort, though she was much frightened by the sight of things, and a good deal appalled at Louis's mad behaviour, of which you have seen something. I think it must be the ergotine that affects his brain at such times.'

The lifesaving drug was a powerful alkaloid that constricted the blood vessels, stemming the haemorrhage. Too much could prove fatal, and it had to be measured out accurately. On one occasion, Fanny had become so agitated that Louis calmly took the glass from her and administered the drug himself. But ergotine also had hallucinogenic properties akin to LSD, leading some fans of *Jekyll and Hyde* to claim the story was conceived as the result of an acid trip. Certainly Louis was off his head as Fanny and Katharine struggled to get the bleeding under control, and some of his requests seemed bizarre, as his wife would relate: 'He is quite rational now, I am thankful to say, but he has just given up insisting that he should be lifted into bed in a kneeling position, his face to the pillow, and then still kneeling he was lifted bodily around, and then a third time held up in the air while he drew in his feet. I never performed a feat as difficult. Every time I expected, if not to kill him, at least to snap his little bones somewhere.'

Thanks to his wife and cousin, Louis survived. But it would be two weeks before he was well enough to risk the journey home to Bournemouth, where Katharine helped lift him out of the carriage and carry him into the sickroom at Skerryvore. There he faced a long and irksome convalescence, again forbidden to speak in the mornings for fear of triggering another horrific outpouring of blood.

Fanny had taken to her bed, leaving him with Katharine for company. Conversation was difficult when he had to write all his answers on a slate, but Katharine could always read to him. Louis loved 'crawlers', as he called horror stories that made the flesh crawl, and his cousin shared his passion for the macabre tales of Edgar Allan Poe. Katharine may have read him *The Fall of the House of Usher*, for two months later it clearly influenced Louis's own crawler *Olalla*, with its Gothic themes of a once-proud noble family in mental decline, preoccupied with death and decay amid the tarnished trappings of nobility in an ancient mansion remote from normal society. And the transformation from Jekyll to Hyde, which came to Louis in a dream while Katharine was at Skerryvore, was foreshadowed by Roderick Usher's song about The Haunted Palace, a metaphor for a healthy, well-ordered mind being taken over by dark thoughts:

> And travellers, now, within that valley,
> Through the red-litten windows see
> Vast forms that move fantastically
> To a discordant melody;
> While, like a ghastly rapid river,
> Through the pale door
> A hideous throng rush out forever,
> And laugh – but smile no more.

In the afternoons, once Louis was permitted to speak, the cousins may have discussed ideas for horror stories of their own. Katharine was fascinated by the idea of one personality being replaced by another within the same body. This led her to write a story called *Through The Red-Litten Windows*, about a feckless young man tricked by a mysterious, beautiful woman into allowing his body and mind to be taken over by another sinister personality. It would not be published until seven years later, but Katharine's story sprang from the same stock as a far more famous tale of duality and may even have played a part in the creation of her cousin's masterpiece.

After three weeks of Gothic horror with Katharine, Louis had the nightmare that would grow into *Strange Case of Dr Jekyll and Mr Hyde*. When Fanny woke him from restless slumber, he reproached her: 'Why did you wake me? I was dreaming a fine bogey tale.' Soon he was feverishly pouring out the story, more than 25,000 words in three days. Fanny, Katharine and 17-year-old Sam tiptoed about the house for fear of disturbing his concentration as a new kind of monster was brought to birth, prefiguring Freudian psychology.

When Louis read them the result, they were shocked – but Fanny, mindful of public opinion now her husband was a famous children's author, suggested he had spoiled the story by making Hyde's depraved behaviour too explicit and that it needed to be more of an allegory. In a fury, Louis flung the manuscript into the fire, got back into bed... and poured out the revised version in another three days.

He now realised there was no need to describe Hyde's vile pleasures, because his readers would be able to imagine them. Six months before *Jekyll and Hyde* appeared, respectable Victorian society had been shaken to the core by a series of articles in the *Pall Mall Gazette*, whose campaigning editor WT Stead was determined to expose the scandal of child prostitution. In the course of his investigation Stead bought a little girl from her mother and sold her to the owner of a brothel, whose customers would pay handsomely to take a child's virginity. At the last moment, Stead would have 'made his excuses and left' with the girl, but not before gathering enough material to paint the most disturbing picture for his readers:

> The innocent girl was taken to a house of ill fame, No. - , P - - - street, Regent-street, where, notwithstanding her extreme youth, she was admitted without question. She was taken up stairs, undressed, and put to bed, the woman who bought her putting her to sleep. She was rather restless, but under the influence of chloroform she soon went over. Then the woman withdrew. All was quiet and still. A few moments later the door opened, and the purchaser entered the bedroom. He closed and locked the door. There was a brief silence. And then there rose a wild and piteous cry – not a loud shriek, but a helpless, startled scream like the bleat of a frightened lamb. And the child's voice was heard crying, in accents of terror, 'There's a man in the room! Take me home; oh, take me home!' And then all once more was still.

Stead's revelations triggered widespread uproar and caused MPs to force a Bill through Parliament, raising the age of consent. All Louis had to do to harness the wave of revulsion that swept through polite drawing-rooms nationwide was to hint at the nature of Hyde's nameless desires. In a casual, brutal encounter on the street, Hyde tramples a child underfoot, like the young girls forced into prostitution in the darker corners of Edinburgh,

London or any city in the land. Thanks to Stead, Louis's readers knew what he meant.

Likewise there was no need to go into detail to describe Hyde's frustration at the repressive, hypocritical society which denied Jekyll his pleasures. In the surviving story Louis simply describes an encounter between Hyde and the MP Sir Danvers Carew – a benevolent do-gooder in the mould of William Ewart Gladstone, who like Louis's father was a rescuer of fallen women. The ensuing murder by lamplight is witnessed by a maid servant at an upstairs window, unable to hear a word of what is said before Hyde erupts with animal rage:

> He had in his hand a heavy cane, with which he was trifling; but he answered never a word, and seemed to listen with an ill-contained impatience. And then all of a sudden he broke out in a great flame of anger, stamping with his foot, brandishing the cane, and carrying on (as the maid described it) like a madman. The old gentleman took a step back, with the air of one very much surprised and a trifle hurt; and at that Mr Hyde broke out of all bounds and clubbed him to the earth. And next moment, with ape-like fury, he was trampling his victim under foot and hailing down a storm of blows, under which the bones were audibly shattered and the body jumped upon the roadway. At the horror of these sights and sounds, the maid fainted.

From such fictional horrors Katharine slipped away to look after a sick friend in Dorking, while keeping up an affectionate correspondence with her cousin: 'Your letter was a great pleasure to me this morning after haunting other sickrooms than yours, dear Louis, for I had been thinking of you in my vigil and your handwriting was a fair sight at dawn!' Her own writing now was purely for money, translating a French book on art into English. *Engraving*, by the Vicomte Henri Delaborde, was meant to be the work of her brother but Bob had failed to make progress. As Katharine wrote in a letter to Louis: 'After language that was maist awfie, and unparalleled angry discussion, a terrible silence as to the position of the Viscount seems to have set in. As Bob is never alluded to by any human creature, I believe he has been goaded into assassinating the Viscount, spurred on probably by the "lone and loathly" Henley or his emissaries.'

Eventually Bob would pay his sister to do the translation, which still appeared under his name, while Katherine downplayed her own contribution: 'Whatever has happened in this matter of the translation I have nothing to do with at all except *en amateur,* if such a word can be used with respect to my long and dreary entanglement with the Viscount. I *know* my work was no good...'

A kind letter from Louis had kept her spirits up and she responded affectionately: 'As you say I know your feeling for me "verra weel" yet I like it written and spoken sometimes as well. I can see you now always pretty well, when I wish to evoke a picture, being just "too weel acquaint" wi' all your low ways and habits from having remained so long at the gates of Skerryvore.' And her love for her cousin was evident as she concluded: 'Now dearest Louis I am yours ever, Katharine de Mattos.'

On returning to London, she managed to find work with the Saturday Review to keep her little family solvent. Louis was doing his best to help sort out her investments and an inheritance which his father, now in declining health, would entrust to him to pass on to Katharine and Bob. With this in mind, Louis was altering his own will to 'choke out de Mattos' from any money Katharine might receive.

On 9 January 1886, *Jekyll and Hyde* sprang upon the unsuspecting Victorian public. As with *Treasure Island*, the writing had come easily and the resulting 'shilling shocker' was an instant sensation. Katharine's copy arrived by post at St Leonard's Terrace with Louis's dedication and the 'lame verses' he had written for her to mark their long affection. It may also have been in recognition of her helping to save his life, and the part she then played in bringing *Jekyll and Hyde* to birth.

Strangely he did not dedicate the book to Fanny, whose criticism had led to the second, toned-down version gracing respectable drawing-rooms worldwide. When Katharine read what Louis had written in her copy, what thoughts ran through her head? And in the years to come did she ever brood over her own little horror tale, left in a desk drawer like a forgotten, less-brilliant cousin of an immortal work of genius?

# 7
# The Red-Litten Windows

THE MANUSCRIPT THAT languished in Katharine's desk drawer is readily recognisable as a relative of *Jekyll and Hyde*. Like Louis's famous story, Katharine's dark tale of duality tells of two people inhabiting one body. Yet it lacks the coherent power of her cousin's version which has the two trading places to enjoy the pleasures of Hyde, liberated by a potion cooked up by the respectable Jekyll. Instead, the anonymous young narrator of *Through The Red-Litten Windows* is lured by a beautiful woman into a scientific experiment. Willingly held captive, the young man witnesses a seemingly lifeless heap wrapped in a cloak being lowered into a room. Katharine, who once helped carry a similar human bundle into Skerryvore after the trip home from Exeter, describes how in an instant the body is vaporised and a spirit released, beginning a sinister process whereby one human being is slowly taken over by another...

## *Through The Red-Litten Windows*
By Katharine De Mattos

### *Out of The Night*

IT was one of those nights of strange, rare beauty, that now and then descend even on London; nights with no darkness at all, when the shimmer of moonlight passes imperceptibly into the radiance of dawn, when night and day are equal forces, or contend only in an exquisite twilight – so gladsome yet tender, one might well wish it eternal. But its influence did not at once calm my unquiet spirit. I had paced long in the wide, tranquil space that fringes the big gates of Regent's Park – to me unknown ground ere the witchery of the night stole softly into my outraged, tortured heart. Thoughts of my brother-in-law, my only relative, in whose care I had been placed when a mere boy, and who had proved himself my bitterest enemy, burned hot within me. His long and carefully planned schemes had succeeded only too well; he had ruined my present and future, and cheated me of my very subsistence. After many underhand manoeuvres, he had at length contrived to put me in the wrong, and so rid himself forever of my presence and my just claims upon him. This very night, goaded to blind fury by his truculent dishonesty and secret baseness, I had flown at his throat and left him half-strangled at my feet. Now, at 19 years of age, I found myself alone in London, a stranger, without a penny in my pocket, and no prospects, not even that of a night's lodging.

I was physically and mentally weary – weary of the havoc within me, and of my purposeless and devious wandering – and glad to pause and take breath a moment. A reaction had begun to set in. My mood was gradually approaching that reckless, effervescent state when one is most open to out-side influences, the stranger the more welcome. Let come what may, was the growing burden of my thoughts, strengthened by the gigantic egotism of youth, which, at great crises, especially at abnormal times and in unfamil-iar places, will make every young man fancy that fate has in store for him special dispensations which shall sweep away the limitations and barriers of ordinary existence. My energies, and impulses, were only too easily roused, and I was apt to forget a certain incapacity to overcome practical difficul-ties which made my brother-in-law sneeringly question my right to rank with the Glorious Company of the Fittest, to which he himself pre-eminently belonged.

As best I might I now dismissed the past with his hideous image from my mind, and suffered the influences of the night to work upon me. It was so rarely beautiful that, late as was the hour, stray wanderers still passed from time to time. Once a carriage rolled by, so near I started, the glimmer of jewels and sheen of whiteness seemed close upon me, and, by the side of the white-robed-figure within, did I indeed see the face of my prostrate brother-in-law glaring upon me from the window? As a falling star flashes and vanishes in a quiet sky, the carriage swept from my sight. A blank fell over the spot; it became as a desert about me...

I leaned against the wall, an indescribable sense of peace stealing over my heart. Instead of anxious plans and thoughts for the future, which might well have beset me, existence seemed but a breath of delight, and I a dream within a dream. I was conscious of the keenest, and at the same time of the vaguest, of sensations, tingling with them to the very fingertips. The breeze that wafted the fragrance of the Park flowers lay cool and kind about me as no other breeze ever did. The silence was unbroken save for the far-off rhythmical measure of a distant policeman advancing and receding on his beat. The distorted past faded to nothingness, the unknown, uncertain future merged itself in the fullness and completeness of a present that seemed every moment growing towards some new and absorbing crisis.

Surely in paradise there never shone a lovelier moon nor a lovelier face than all at once drew out of the blue distance and stood motionless before me. There is a beauty that strikes us dumb, that, once and for ever, makes us feel that the word is profaned or inadequate. It is not always in a woman's form that such beauty is found; when it is, the sight is perhaps more perturbing than rejoicing. It creates an undefinable yet ever increasing hunger, rather than the mere anguish to have and to hold. The longing to gaze perpetually rather than approach, the looking for something beyond and above it, as though the visible beauty were but the outward expression of a more transcendent, far-off loveliness, are the predominating feelings. You may have glimpses of this disquieting sort in a passing face or form, and wish for no more than a glimpse. Beauty of this type belongs of right to no concrete person or place. It should be seen in snatches, on the wing; flashing here and there its mystical significance.

To see it as I saw it emerge like a vision of the night and stand before me was nearly as disconcerting as it was exhilarating. The radiance of that loveliness has, I am certain, never been surpassed – in one woman, at least. Her hair was of that exceeding depth of glory that no dimness may rob of its colour. In the shadowy moonlight it glowed and burned as though in perfect day, and the drooping eyes were as lamps lighting the exquisite contour and pallor of the face. Yet it evoked in me none of the glamour called love at first sight. It was too impersonal, perhaps too perfect and dazzling for that, and it showed not one ray of warmth or kindness to cheer the dreary splendour. I could not tell wherein lay the perfection, nor yet the inadequacy of the charm; I only knew it was not the sort of beauty we call human here on earth. Yet this woman's presence stirred me to the heart, though only with that sudden hunger after perfectness that is latent in all of us, the recognition that the seen is but the shadow of that unseen and intangible something towards which we all our lives stretch our hands.

When she spoke her voice had something of the quality of her beauty; it sounded the music of eternity, not time; it recalled no place, class, nor country. In themselves the words were commonplace enough.

'I want you to do something for me,' she said, in a tone which showed that into her mind there entered no thought of possible hesitation in a hearer.

It was regal, passionless, betraying neither anxiety nor other feeling. Yet I thrilled and responded to it, not in words – at first I found none – but with every impulse and nerve of my body. All the recklessness and love of adventure in my nature were aflame at once. Brought face to face with so romantic a situation, it was not likely I should take time to reflect. I only bowed my head in silent yet eager assent, and in longing to hear the voice once more. With a gesture unspeakably graceful and commanding, she pointed to a house across the road, distinguished in no way from those about it except that brilliant lights still burned in most of its windows.

'You must come with me,' she continued, 'I want help; in that house lies one at the point of death. You may have to get help, give aid – in short, I know not what may be necessary, but there is no one at hand to do what may be required. I can rely on you?'

She paused, turning upon me the full splendour of her eyes, till then slightly veiled, not so much deprecating my willingness as stating a fact which, for her, had neither import nor interest except in so far as it might affect the desired service. My answer came then, came abundantly, in words of wholesale surrender, moonlit madness, reckless defiance of fate and my own responsibility. I told her I was at nobody's bidding, not my own even. Identity, personality, future – I could lay claim to none of these. No one, not myself even, would need my services. She might use or misuse me as she liked.

'Make of me what you please,' I cried, with all the exaggerated emphasis of youth. 'You see in me a shell, an empty husk, a tabernacle swept and garnished; people it as you please, summon what spirits you desire, I will do their bidding.'

She only let her steady, brilliant gaze rest upon me till my eager words failed and faltered and ceased altogether. They left her so absolutely cold and detached that my cynical lightness fell abashed before the icy indifference of her manner. In it was no trace of wonder, reproach, of the womanly pity I half-unconsciously expected my words to evoke.

'There will be nothing to take you away, I *believe*.'

She spoke in measured, thoughtful accents, as though whatever peculiarity or misfortune might be in my life they could, in themselves, be as nothing to her. Then she again fell silent, musing, as though the idea of this complete self-surrender, this absolute isolation of a fellow creature, fitted well with her own plan of action. No man – not even the young man who nourishes 'a youth sublime' on visions of the amazing condescensions of unknown

duchesses – could harbour the thought that the charm of his own personality was for anything in the case. I was only the convenient circumstance,
the lucky occasion, and I knew it. Yet if that young man were like me, what
would he not do or dare only to see such beauty live and breathe a moment
longer? I lived, I know, in expectation and suffering, when she turned from
me and moved to a street lamp to consult a written paper as though for
instruction and guidance. I feared she might, on second thoughts, be about
to decline my impulsive self-surrender as disproportionate or impertinent.
Not so; once more she flashed upon me the incredible delight of her presence, once more the colourless, magical voice sang in my ears like the morning stars together.

'Come, then, come at once,' and she walked at my side, not leading the
way as a meaner majesty might. She did not again speak, however, and she
once more veiled her eyes, not from the importunity of mine – that she no
more heeded than the far-off heavens heed the foolish stargazers beneath –
but evidently in thought or perplexity. In less than a minute we arrived at
the house she had pointed out; noiselessly she slid a key, and, opening the
door, signed to me to follow, shutting it very quietly behind us. The house
was intensely still, for all the brilliant lights that burned in it. Not pausing
a moment, she opened a door to the left and passed in, I following in her
wake. The moment was fraught with anxiety; I felt myself tremble, but only,
curiously enough, lest her beauty should prove a thing born of the night and
the wavering shadows, and fade away under the hard gaslight flaring on us
from several brackets. It only burned the brighter.

There was no one in the room. The walls were covered with pictures, and
but for them it might have looked bare. Certainly the furniture was plentiful,
even luxurious, but not a stray book, bit of work, nor any sort of knick-knack
served to show whether the occupant was young or old, male or female, and
yet the place wore an indescribable air of having been lately tenanted. It was
as though stray materials and small personal effects had been disposed of in
a hasty but effectual sweep. The contrast with the well-covered walls was
the greater. Large vases holding tall flowering plants of faint pale hues stood
about in the corners and in the windows. Beside the couch, in one of these,
was a table spread with fine damask, an antique wine flagon, a curious drinking goblet, and various sorts of meats. Folding doors half hid, half revealed a
sleeping chamber beyond. All this I perceived hurriedly, carelessly, as a man
makes note of objects and places he never expects to look on again.

'You will oblige me by staying here just now, whatever happens or does not happen. Your help may be required. On the other hand, it may not be needed, but your presence, for a time, we must have. Do not refrain from sleep if it overtakes you. You can be awakened, if need be. In the meantime... Be fed and comforted!'

With a smile, the first and the last I saw on her face, she pointed with a gesture of invitation towards the table and the couch; and so saying left me.

## 'Twixt Sleeping and Waking

I HAD hardly realised how exhausted I was till she spoke, and it was not till I had well eaten and drunk of the pleasant unknown wine in the flagon that I felt how greatly I had needed refreshment. Then I was glad to throw myself on the couch and meditate. Stretched there at ease, every detail of the unfamiliar place gradually worked upon my attention till I knew I should never forget what I looked upon as merely a piquant and passing acquaintance. There is always something provoking in this mechanical involuntary attention to inanimate things. Ere the colour of the walls, the pictures, the hue of the carpet, even an irregular crack or fissure on the ceiling, had fixed themselves on my brain, I began to speculate vaguely but persistently as to what sort of person – of what age, sex, manner of life – owned the rooms; and these ideas I pursued to the exclusion of the problems which should naturally have possessed me.

The question of my own future I had already cast to the winds as something not belonging to me, as cancelled. My life seemed now to date from the present episode, yet the strange undeveloped situation, the possible grief or anxiety of the beautiful stranger, even the fate of the unknown moribund troubled my sympathy or imagination, so far, very little. Only a dull aching in the temples, the sense of a stupefied vigil that I, or someone who had been I, was forced to hold, pressed on me gradually and succeeded to my intense interest in trivial surroundings. My eyes grew heavier and more leaden, yet I was not sleepy in the ordinary sense of the word. I did not doze off, nor forget my whereabouts. Possibly the deep, all-pervading stillness prevented this. A stillness so weighty and oppressive as possessed that house I have never before experienced. A spell of silence, strong as death itself, brooded over it. The busy streets of London lay fathoms deep in slumber, the rare slumber that holds them so short a space. Only the ceaseless, still small voice of a clock in a hidden place, pulsated like a heart that watches and counts the footfalls of an unknown fear or danger. It was as though I, too, unknowing and unreasoning, were forced to wait and watch, perhaps to share in an event drawing ever nearer.

Suddenly the stillness broke, the small voice of the clock was drowned in a louder noise. Something approached the house, feet stumbled up the steps to the front door, making the hush within seem closer and deeper. A man's voice outside spoke distinctly and, as it were, close in my ear, and to my excited sense the voice sounded like the voice of my brother-in-law.

'This is the house, it is certainly the house.' He paused; then added, 'We ought to be present ourselves to make assurance doubly sure.'

A hand stole to the knocker; I knew it was raised for it vibrated ever so slightly, though no sound followed. Still cautiously it crept to the window, the window where I lay, and fumbled about as though to raise the sash. My late indifference passed rapidly into fear. Then another voice spoke in lower tones, but the sense of the words did not reach me. A sick pause followed, a whispered parley, and the sound of retreating footsteps.

Once more that death-like silence fell over everything but the tumultuous throbbing of my own pulses, joined to the regular beat of the clock, and a nameless, unreasoning horror that grew quick upon me. Then a soothing stupor partially overcame me, quenching for a time the painful renewal and quickening of my dormant faculties. I lay back as I had lain – how long I knew not, an exceeding weight of languor, an oppression of weariness rather than ordinary drowsiness once more upon me, with I know not what added sense of remoteness and distance from all about me. To myself I seemed to sleep, to dream... I fell, or seemed to fall, from towering heights to immeasurable depths, borne on billows of visible slumber, and yet my present whereabouts remained to some extent always a fixed point. What time passed is impossible to say, for all sense of it was obliterated in the seeming vastness about me...

Presently I roused a little, the silence grew alive and agitated with sounds of sibilant whisperings, when, as yet, the whisperers were unseen. To my exceeding amazement, rather than fear, the ceiling gently parted at the fissure I had noted, exposing a yawning twilight gulf above. From this a something, not yet definable, was lowered to the floor with the utmost care and precision. It lay at a distance from my couch, a shape at which I shuddered, scarce knowing why. My brain continued to work, but my physical helplessness was now complete, and everything but the nerves of sight and hearing seemed paralysed. Almost simultaneously with the lowering of the burden, the door by which I had entered opened, and gave passage to several persons, all of whom gazed at me in turn, as though to satisfy themselves as to my condition before passing to the far end of the room. With them was the beautiful stranger; her face was the only one known to me, the only one I could have recognised. While the men bent over the lowered burden she approached the couch, and once more scanned my face with that grave solicitude so unmistakably not for my own sake.

Then took place, as it were, at my elbow, a scene inexplicably yet vividly real, a scene which by some curious optical effect appeared miles away, yet had all the distinctness of objects seen through the small end of an old-fashioned opera glass. This clearness of detail and the quickness and coherency in all I saw done forbade me to look on it as a fevered dream. What passed was *done*, not imagined, and had it not been for the weight of that which possessed me, and the impassive yet perfect sway of the woman's beauty, I should assuredly have sprung to my feet and released myself from the fearful spell. To shut my eyes was as impossible as to move. Look I must, watch I was compelled.

It was not a heap, but a figure that the men were now engaged in carefully huddling on to some sort of support or stand: a man's figure that fell about with horrid limpness, yet with a certain painful rigidity. It was habited in the ample folds of a loose falling cloak. The face was then, and afterwards, turned from me. I do not know whether an unmirthful laugh escaped me, but as I gazed at the grotesque, Guy Fawkes-like figure in a sort of fascinated dismay, it seemed to me that in size and general outline it was like me; the back of the head and the hair, of somewhat uncommon colour and luxuriance, were certainly like mine. It might have been my own effigy I thus saw fixed and tortured into this semblance of humanity. Was it a lay figure I saw, a mannikin of some sort, or a human being in the grip of an unnatural, an enforced trance? Was I myself drugged, dead, or what?

At this point I am not certain that a discordant laugh did not break from my lips and startle the men at their work; they glanced up at me sharply, and a dreary echo of laughter sounded from somewhere. Villainy, unknown, horrible villainy was at work – in the very air. I made an impotent effort to move, my lips writhed in inarticulate speech, but no words came. The beautiful creature at my side only moved to force a few drops of the fluid from the flagon between my lips, then pressed her fingers firmly on them, and on my eyes, murmuring – 'Peace, peace'. The pressure quieted while it lasted, but it was the bliss of agony that held me still. When she removed her touch I stared about me, half expecting to find everything vanished like the phantasmagoria of a dream.

But now the figure was bound into an erect position. Once more they bent over it, consulting together in low tones, a wrought yet eager expression on every face. Fear clutched at me and nearly took my breath away, for it was then borne in on me that this was no dead but a living fellow creature, entranced by foul means, whose latent life they were about to take in some blood-curdling fashion. Not so – not at once at least. For a while they stood aloof from it united in their purpose, clustering about the table, opening and shutting cases, passing phials and globules from hand to hand in a quick and dexterous manner. A spirit lamp was prepared and lighted. Then followed renewed and careful assorting of more liquids and substances that burnt up with a sudden flare, and died down gurgling. All this time one man was giving directions to the rest, consulting notes and a watch with all his energy and thought concentrated in his face. It was an anxious, delicate task, judging from the care with which they avoided unnecessary contact with their materials, and it seemed a relief to them all when this part of their task ended.

Once more they came and clustered about the figure – the figure that looked like me. Gently they felt and pressed it all over, as though testing its consistency and fitness to be operated upon. Seemingly the examination satisfied them. A long, syringe-like tube, in connection with what looked like a small battery, was charged. The crisis was approaching. The man who had throughout taken the lead stepped forward and focussed the figure in the region of the heart. All grew pale and blinded their eyes, except the chief operator. The woman still remained at my side, but her inhuman, inexorable beauty was turned from me. Her face rested on the cushions, her hands were pressed to her ears. A sharp, light report vibrated through the room, shivering a globe and splintering a mirror. An instant's quiver, and upheaval of the bound figure, and all was still. Only where it had been nothing – the entire fabric had vanished. A body had been made invisible, obliterated; a something, a spirit, had been set at large, liberated. I knew not; my strained vision relaxed, consciousness deserted me, and I lay back, free myself, for a space, of thought and time.

## *What Place is This – And Who Am I In It?*

LIFE has few more sickening moments, sleeping or waking, than those that herald the return of memory to half-forgotten misery. I cannot say how long it was ere I came to myself in the spot where consciousness had deserted me. I was but dimly aware of my whereabouts and antecedents, aware chiefly of a sensation of physical ease and vague *bien-être* like the expression of ordinary convalescence. Infinite peace succeeding to infinite pain was the predominating sensation. Out of a swarm of past visions, loathly or lovely, the present began to emerge, a solid reality in which my whereabouts seemed in a way familiar, yet new and strange.

It must have been early evening when I thus 'came back'. The veiled lustre of sunset struggled faintly into darkened places, and crept athwart low-drawn roseate blinds, showing through the wide turned-back doors, the dim vista of a room beyond. The breeze hardly stirred the white faces of the clematis flowers that stood steadfastly watching, as though for something that must come. The mere sight of them disturbed me, and brought back a train of remembrances I dreaded to pursue... Everything about me seemed carefully and well ordered. Outward comfort at least was mine, in lieu of miserable and nameless confusion. My brain groped feebly for comprehension, my bodily eyes strove to take in further details. Recollection was fast returning, faint still, but increasingly clear and painful.

Mine was then no pleasant convalescence, no respite from fever-stricken visions only. Some event since leaving my brother-in-law had certainly taken place, something besides an illness. I was the man who had witnessed, not dreamed, things unspeakable, impossible to utter. Something urged me to flee somewhere, anywhere, away from this dreadful spot – to denounce someone, anyone. Beyond this my mind did not travel. My weakness and confusion of thought were still so great that a swimming in my sight and a buzzing in my ears were my reward when I strove to move, or even to think out my thoughts. A merciful oblivion once more overtook me, and blotted out the scene.

I woke again stronger, with thoughts more collected and coherent. A gentle footfall sounded, a woman entered, a servant of everyday aspect, bearing a small tray. She approached to give me nourishment, and seeing me at length conscious of her presence, began to speak with much propriety of tone and manner. How soothing yet baffling the way in which the prosaic and abnormal are blended!

'I was to let you know, sir,' she began, 'As soon as you were stronger and more able to "take notice", that this house changed hands during your illness. You were too ill to be moved, and my mistress, in taking the house, was asked to see after you. She has been told your tastes and manner of living, and I was to let you know that everything will go on as before. There are no other lodgers; you will not be put out of your way.'

It was a longish speech, clear enough in import, yet it was amazement that made me silent and acquiescent. The house has changed hands. 'Everything will go on as before!' The commonplace words and manner staggered me. Was she feigning, or really ignorant of the plot and of all that had come and gone in this very house, and of my true identity? The house was, I felt, only, indeed, too surely under the same influences, whatever outward changes had been wrought, or appearances assumed. Not from her – possibly because not in her power – should I get any explanation of the state of the case. Possibly a mistake or misapprehension of some sort was at the bottom of a part of the drama, and an explanation might yet follow. But it must come without help from me! So far I could do nothing.

The woman continued to nurse me while it was necessary, and to wait upon me afterwards. Before long it seemed that something of my former health returned. The subdued quiet of the house, if mysterious, was just then agreeable. Nothing disturbed, nothing jarred; it was quiet cultivated to an art. Perhaps to it I owed my slow recovery, as after a great shock, we must recover strength, if only to meet renewed suffering. Were it not for nature's recuperative processes how could the brain bear the quick torture, the fitful fever of living?

I bethought me to ask for the mistress of the house, to find out what doctor, if any, had attended me, that, by questions to both, I might learn something of the circumstances in which I now found myself involved. But the impenetrability of the 'well-trained servant' was in this case so deep-seated that I merely gathered that her mistress was a semi invalid, who took little part in the management of the house. My interview with her led to less even than I expected. I found her in an upper room, a tall, silent person with a senile smile, who would have seemed in her dotage but for a trick her eyes had of lightening and darkening in a vigilant, unpleasant fashion. To make her understand, or seem to understand, any part of my statement or questions, was hopeless. The currents of her brain appeared frozen to new impressions. She scarcely listened when I talked, but maundered on to herself in an absent kind of way, now seeming to realise my presence, then to forget it. Clearly nothing was to be gained from her, and I made no further attempt in that direction.

As yet I was scarce fit to pass beyond the rooms, which, while they repelled, fascinated me. I lived like one expecting a summons, a dismissal, or explanation. None came. I felt I might one day have to give an account, not only of my stewardship, but of the monstrous circumstances that had led to it. Where, or to whom to carry my preposterous story? More and more I shrank from speech, even from thought about the past. A petrifying influence was at work upon me. I was growing to the place like a limpet to the rock. I even detected about me unseen determined influences forcing me, as it seemed, to assume the identity of the deceased. My position was unnatural, intolerable, yet it relieved me from immediate action, from anxiety as to a future with which I was ill able to cope. A spring in me was broken, my native impetuosity and love of adventure were forever scotched. Though I at length fell into some sort of forced quiescence, I was miserably haunted by the feeling that I had stepped into the place of another personality I dreaded to think upon. I wondered if I had really seen and heard, or only imagined I saw and heard, my brother-in-law on two bygone occasions, and if he were alive or dead – in any case, that chapter of my life was closed. I recalled the iron-bound smile with which he used to deprecate my want of strength, of purpose, my lack of what he called 'staying power'. Now my very identity, career, and personality seemed indeed annihilated. Another man's had been infamously and fatally made ready; into them I had unwittingly stepped, and where was issue or escape to be found? Defiantly, jestingly, I had in an evil moment thrown myself, as the sport and toy of circumstance, on chance and on the world; how should I redeem myself? I had cast from me what, at the time, seemed to my distorted imagining a useless and worthless destiny, instead of the sacred, mysterious responsibility it in reality was. It was lost, indeed; whose, whose had I found? Is existence, then, really the hand-to-hand struggle we hear of, where the places are so precious as to be seized as soon as vacant, though their owners fight for them with tears and blood?

One of the many explanations I offered myself was, that a band of persons leagued together for purposes of their own, of which my brother-in-law was aware, had secured me to his and their profit, and that my presence was necessary to conceal the disappearance of a victim. This was the one clear thing in the matter. In any case I was utterly, entirely alone, for the myriads of London may be as a vast and teeming desert about one. It was so with me. Not a face, not at voice from the past reached me, and how I feared yet longed for them! I sometimes felt that if only once, for a moment, I might unburden myself in the ear of a fellow creature I should go less heavily laden. I believe I got the length of calling on a magistrate or functionary of some sort. But before I had got far in my story, the difficulty of speaking grew insurmountable. It seemed too strange, too abnormal a tale to recount, with his grave scrutiny, his matter-of-fact, courteous manner bearing upon me. Was he, I wonder, divided betwixt the notions that I was some graceless youth working off a charge or mystification upon him, or a deserving lunatic training for bolt and bar? I could not tell. I went back to my destination by a roundabout way, feeling more unreal, more haunted than ever, and tortured with the thought that I was watched – back to the life that was not mine, yet seemed but certainly the only one open to me.

## The Two in One

THE dim, quiet rooms never seemed natural but with the summer twiiight falling about them. I would sit then, or pace the floor for long together – alone. Alone, how should I be otherwise? What in the midst of multitudes could I hope for but one unbroken solitude? And yet I began to feel not really alone. Therein lay the sting, the horror of the situation. In all my seeming loneliness I was not really alone. I felt encompassed, haunted by an invisible presence.

Thoughts of the body that had disappeared, of the spirit that had been liberated, had so often filled my mind, that its actual though invisible presence seemed but too often with me. Was I but the wraith of myself, and he the true reality ranging at large, and seeking a way by which to make himself known? Camping on his ground, tenanting his very abode, what might I not expect to see or hear? Was it true, or some horrid fancy that I now began to find myself developing thoughts and habits that seemed not mine, but someone else's? Was it indeed, by my own wish or another's that I often for moments together stopped to inhale the faint perfume of the clematis? Why, too, should I cling to the gloom and quiet of twilight; I who had once loved it but for its contrast to the stir and brightness of morning?

Groping one day with idle fingers I came upon the photograph of a man stuck behind a mirror. It was blurred and dim, but the uncommon pose of the figure – leaning with averted face on a broken pillar – was plain enough. It affected me strangely, for in it I recognised the never-to-be-forgotten figure I had seen that night, and the sight gave fresh impetus and vigour to my growing imaginings. Had the man no face, or one too horrible for view? In an access of repugnance I tore the picture to little pieces, and scattered them – not so the impression. It grew and flourished. Here was I kept in life by means of the annihilation of this very person. Here was I growing hourly less myself and more incorporate with him in an unfamiliar and as yet imperfect partnership. Would our existence henceforth be an ignoble struggle between the remnant of my castaway self and his unseen emanation, striving so desperately to force its presence upon me, perhaps to drain the very breath from my being?

Sometimes it was as though I, myself, stood quivering on the threshold and confines of another's spirit, only to be drawn back by the remaining chords of my own identity and consciousness. At other times I felt it would be his part to make the plunge, and no words can express the terror the idea gave me. It was as though I had impiously trifled with a natural, unwritten law, and laid myself bodily and spiritually naked and open to the workings of unseen, unimagined forces. Something like a continual pulling one against the other, a struggle of rival powers was going on, a struggle in which no stable equilibrium seemed possible. In so hideous a warfare, with a mind so divided, how may one stand?

Thinking thus, I gazed into the mirror at my haggard, questioning reflection, as though I almost expected to see it transformed to the unknown lineaments of the man, in the shuffling off of whose body I had unconsciously helped. Fixedly I gazed, actually expecting the astounding manifestation to begin – the spectacle in which I should behold a disembodied, hungry spirit striving to re-clothe itself in my own flesh and blood, to proclaim the deed that had hurried it to its doom. I started fearfully. I had only caught a glimpse of the back of my own head and shoulders imaged in another mirror. Much shaken, I sat down and mused, as on many a weary or fearful twilight before.

The windows were open, but the night was so airless that the clematis flowers only trembled slightly, like faces of palsied age. Setting the street door ajar I placed myself so that I could hear the approach of any one in that quiet thoroughfare. Suddenly there smote upon me a great longing for the sight of a warm human face, the sound of a human voice, instead of the pallid and intolerable existence I shared with the dead. This night my position seemed to hold me in a less awesome grip than usual. I could almost see the lonely, the pathetic side, to the exclusion of the more awful aspect it generally presented. If only some touch of sympathy might reach and once more link me with the living, working world, become now like a dim and distant pageant!

Far down the street a child's voice and patter of footsteps sounded pleasantly. Only echoes from the lives of others could, I knew, reach me, yet this one night I would listen, this one night hope. The feet drew nearer and – oh, joy of life! – they paused before the house, they climbed the steps, pattering uncertainly, hurriedly along the passage. I heard a child's voice audibly persuading some older person to enter the room in a language I did not understand. Then straight to me where I sat in the deepening shadows came a young child, leading, yet led by an old black attendant.

With a glad cry that seemed to slay the besetting phantoms, she sprang to me, exclaiming: 'I have come back to you. Come back, oh so far! Are you not pleased to have me again?'

Was it possible that she mistook me for him, the real owner of the place? For my life I dared not break the spell. I could but hide my face, and encourage the glad illusion that was to bring to me the very voice and touch I had been longing for.

'Pleased!' I murmured. 'My child, I cannot tell you how pleased.'

At the first sound of my voice the little creature raised its head and started away from me in wrath and fear. 'Ah! who, *who* are you? You are not he. I am blind, I cannot see; but you are not my friend, the good little father whom without seeing I loved. Wicked man, say, say, where is he?'

Her voice rose in passionate sorrow and anger, and tears, the first I had shed since childhood, forced their way from my own eyes. They fell for her, perhaps for myself, for love, for the unknown, untasted joy of life, and all the cruelties and pangs of existence. To lose this flower of hope just as it budded was hell. Her tones changed:

'Oh, poor man, you are crying for him, too; then you have no one to love you either. But I will stay and love you always.'

Again her fingers crept to my face, her cheek was set to mine, and so for a moment she pressed the lonely horror from my heart. Not for long, O God, not for long!

At once, and not without surprise, I had guessed her to be the child of the beautiful stranger, though of her own circumstances and parentage she knew nothing. Her face was almost as beautiful as the face of the woman; but it had, besides, the exquisite beauty of kindness the other lacked. Somehow I could not fear her, though I readily guessed the man she sought and the being who haunted me were identical. I only felt that she and I were together involved in a common mystery, whose mazes were inscrutable and past finding out.

She and the black woman took up their abode in the house, and neither by word nor sign was allusion made to their coming in that strange dwelling. More than ever I now felt bound to it, for one link that held me was forged of human love and pity. For perfect liberty I almost felt I could not have deserted those silent rooms, gladdened at times by her voice. I loved her as one in a dungeon loves the slender ray of light that visits and blesses him. In the terrors of my worst haunted moments, plagued in my dawn and uprising by the importunity of the being whose place I held, the blind child stood often and radiantly between.

It was when alone, or in the streets, that I was now most haunted. Once at a swarming crossing, blocked with traffic, a voice in my ear distinctly whispered,

'Who are you? Dear gentleman, do you know who you are? Take care; have a care.'

A soft, mocking laugh poisoned the air. Eagerly I turned and scanned the street. The crowd was once more in motion, a moving sea about me. The whisper was lost as soon as uttered; its source I knew not, but the words echoed in my ears. At home they came and haunted me, giving to the invisible presence the voice it had till then lacked. Like the atmosphere it remained unseen, yet it weighed on me at every pore.

I began to think I sometimes discerned the vague outline, the shadow of a shape, the face always turned from me. At other times it appeared to stand thoughtfully gazing into space, then to turn, but always without revealing its features, or, if it did, changed and dissolved as though reflected in troubled waters. I argued with myself that all this was conjured up by the scenes I had witnessed, and yet – against reason – I felt that an influence which could struggle thus desperately must sooner or later conquer. I wanted to know what this man had been, if a fiend in human shape, or one who had known something of the joys and graces of life. To me his mind was a *tabula rasa*, and I cannot say how this ignorance terrified me. Would annihilation of my own consciousness come gradually, or would I burst with a shock into the silent sea of his? Often I have felt on the verge of a metamorphosis, or of witnessing a manifestation on his part, when the entrance of the child would for the time scatter the impression. Thus in her frail, blind beauty she grew beside me, and as dawn or twilight I found her very fair. ·

One night I had been more than usually loath to see her and the black woman depart, but at length they were gone, and I alone with the shadows. At once the power of the presence asserted itself. I rose and paced the floor; voiceless and featureless it met me, and paced beside me. I flung myself again in a chair; it leaned over the back with me. Unable to bear the steady oppression longer, I moved to the mantelshelf and gazed at my own reflection. The pale image stared back at me, and I noted its ravages. Was I really to see my own face dwindle before my eyes to make way for those other unknown lineaments? I gazed into the hunted, imploring eyes that seemed to gloom and waver at me. The shadow of something flitted across them. Was the dread change beginning? I looked again. *It had come. The face was his. Was it also mine?* A fearful longing to obliterate the awful duality of the being came upon me. Did it not, with its own eyes, implore pity and deliverance at my hands? O Christ, the feeling mastered me! My fingers stole round the neck. I seized the throat with both hands to quench its damnable life, the iniquitous joint horror of both our lives. A gurgling sounded in my ears; the wide-opened eyes rolled madly...

Then arms – soft arms – not his nor mine – came winding about me, unclasping my murderous grip. Who was it climbing unsteadily on the chair, gently disengaging my frenzied fingers? Child, or angel, it was you, once more, you who destroyed that horrible reality or phantasy. And I loved you, loved you with a new rapture born of terror and despair. May all else perish! To live for you, care for you, lend my life and my eyes for you, was my one thought. For you, too, loved me. This much was true, and surely no nightmare! True that we – not he and I – were one on that mad glad night. No dream that you were in an hour grown to a tall, fair lily, with beauty human yet divine, not cruel as hers. Little Love, the spring came and slew the dark dreams, and set us free! Was it sweet sleep or a swoon still sweeter that fell so softly upon us?

They have taken her away. I am alone once more in that accursed place, the home of fiends and 'evil things in robes of sorrow' who mock and whisper at me. As of old the hateful twilight falls apace, and shadows lie deep and dark around. The white-faced clematis flowers beleaguer and nod at me as in many a teeming vision. My brain must burst, my soul must away. Out, out into the streets crowded and frantic with the pains and pleasures of millions I rush. The more crowded, the more furious, the better for me.

A carriage is close upon me. How madly it tears along, bearing you in it, my blind child. Yes, there she sits with closed eyes, not seeing, but dreaming of me; and by her side the beautiful woman who destroyed me. She sees me, and points at the child with her cruel, quiet grace. But she dares not smile at me this time, she dares not! And she shall not keep the child from me. I will reach her though I tear out the woman's heart; though these horses that rear and prance upon me with their flaming eyes were the deathless horses themselves, they should not keep her from me!

A hospital nurse and doctor stand gazing down on the bed where a young man lies. Her intelligent expression grows soft and sympathetic as she makes her report. His is keenly attentive.

'It is a remarkable face,' he says, musingly, in reply to some comment. 'And you say, nurse, he has not really rested since they brought him in from the Regent's Park?'

'No, sir, it is pitiful to hear him; nothing quiets him much. He just wanders incessantly among fearful sights and sounds till I am weary and terrified as I listen. 'Tis like living years and years, wandering miles and miles.'

The surgeon listened yet more attentively, then bent to touch the patient's brow.

'He will have a long rest presently,' he muttered.

# 8

# An Uneasy Friendship

EXACTLY WHEN *Through The Red-Litten Windows* was written is not known, although the idea dates from the time at Skerryvore when Louis gave birth to *Jekyll and Hyde*. If his masterpiece came first, it is easy to assume Katharine was simply seeking to emulate his success. Yet between publication of Louis's story and her own, a change in their relationship would make any suggestion of copying her cousin or trading on his famous name an anathema. By publishing her story under a pseudonym, she would avoid any reader making the link with *Jekyll and Hyde*.

Unlike Louis or Fanny, Katharine struggled to get her work published and a delay of seven years would not be out of the ordinary. So if her story dates back to the time in the sickroom at Skerryvore when *Jekyll and Hyde* was born, was it inspired by her cousin's tale of duality – or might his story have been inspired in part by hers? It is impossible to say, but the tricky question of writers copying each other's ideas did loom large when Katharine, whom Fanny now liked to think of as her best friend, wrote a story shortly afterwards about a young man on a train who meets a strange girl apparently escaped from an asylum. Unlike the beautiful but cruel woman in *Through The Red-Litten Windows*, the girl turns out to be a benevolent creature, bringing about the young man's salvation by challenging his comfortable, predictable life.

Louis by now was busy, when his health allowed, with a new novel that would emerge as *Kidnapped*, so Katharine asked Henley instead for his opinion on her manuscript. He was impressed and sent it to several editors, but each time it was returned with a rejection slip. To Henley's chagrin, it seemed his recommendation was not enough to get the story published.

Occasionally Louis was well enough to spend a few days in London, where the Stevensons and Katharine might meet up with Henley at his home in Shepherd's Bush. The talk there turned to Katharine's rejected tale, and Henley produced the manuscript he had been unable to sell. Immediately it excited the attention of Fanny, who as a published author with her name on *The Dynamiter* now felt qualified to advise others on their work. When a nervous young woman called Adelaide Boodle had come to the door of Skerryvore, hoping Mr Stevenson might deign to help her with her writing, Fanny had told her she would look at it instead as Louis was very busy. But the great man's cousin may have been less willing to accept the patronage of his wife. Katharine was no longer a novice and was making a living by her pen at the *Saturday Review* – a fact acknowledged by Louis in rather luke-warm terms when he wrote to its editor, Walter Pollock: 'I hear my cousin Mrs de Mattos is doing some work for you; I trust she may please you; she is too great a friend of mine for me to have an opinion.'

Pollock may have been one of those who turned down Katharine's story, but Louis made no mention of this, nor what he thought of the tale himself. Fanny was enthusiastic and thought she could improve on the narrative. If Katharine could not get it published, would she mind if Fanny used the idea herself, turning the girl into a shape-shifting watersprite or nixie? Had Katharine been a plain-speaking American, she would simply have replied in the negative. Had Fanny been a native of polite, understated Edinburgh, she would never have construed her best friend's hesitant reply as consent. As it was, the awkward moment passed and the story was quietly dropped. Louis continued to be charming and very good company, while Katharine secretly adored him.

Like her cousin she could be amusing without revealing her true feel-ings, a characteristic he acknowledged in a letter: 'My dear Katharine, 'Tis the most complete *blague* and folly to write to you; you never answer and, even when you do, your letters crackle under the teeth like ashes; containing nothing, as they do, but unseasonable japes and a great cloudy vagueness as of the realms of chaos. In this I know well they are like mine; and it becomes me well to write such – but not you – for reasons too obvious to mention... Of your views, state, finances, etc, etc, I know nothing. We were mighty near the end of all things financially, when a strange shape of a hand giving appeared in Heaven or from Hell, and set us up again for the moment; yet still we totter on a whoreson brink. I beg parding – I forgot I was writing to a lady; but the word shall stay: it is the only word; I would say it to the Q___n of E_____d.'

In fact Louis's literary success was growing and, with 40,000 copies of *Jekyll and Hyde* sold already, his finances were far healthier than his cousin's. But exhaustion had forced him to end *Kidnapped* in mid-air, leaving David Balfour on the steps of the British Linen Bank in Edinburgh with half the story yet untold. By the time serialisation finished in July 1886 and advance royalties were coming in for the book, Louis needed rest. Kindly Katharine took the teenage Sam away on holiday to the Scilly Isles, with Snoodie and Coggie Ferrier. Sam was never fond of children, but he might find Coggie entertaining, and his absence gave Louis and Fanny a break. To keep him amused in the 'Silly Isles', Louis sent his stepson a parcel containing an empty matchbox, an empty cigarette-paper book, a bell from a cat's collar, an iron kitchen spoon and a lump of coal. The look of bewilderment on the boy's face would at least have made Katharine smile, and the holiday with Coggie led to a lifelong friendship between the two women.

While the historical romance of *Kidnapped* was being praised by the critics, a different kind of fiction was emerging in France. Although Louis recognised the genius of Emile Zola, he found the Frenchman's grim realism ugly and deplorable. A year previously, Zola had published his masterpiece *Germinal*, set in a poor French mining community which becomes a hotbed of socialism when the desperate miners go on strike. Zola was conscious of being on an ideological mission when he wrote what he called *ce sacré bouquin* (this sacred book) but Louis, and it seems Katharine, did not take it quite so seriously. What, they wondered, would have been the result if Zola had written about Bournemouth instead, whose inhabitants were not miners but genteel invalids nursing their illnesses behind net curtains? This led to a humorous correspondence between the cousins in which Bournemouth seemingly became 'Illingsworth'. Years later Henley would recall it as 'a comic Zolaism – *Ce Sacré Illingsworze*, or words to that effect – the fun of which consisted largely, if not wholly, in the application of Zola's distemperate and exorbitantly lecherous view of art and life to Bournemouth'.

Most of the letters were written by Katharine before going off to the Scilly Isles. Louis mentioned them in a letter to Henley, who responded: 'Your praise of Katharine's letters gave me an idea. Don't you think the correspondence might be redacted into a sort of comic *nouvelle*?' But despite Henley's persistent interest – 'Are those letters of Katharine's any good? This is the third time of asking' – the idea was never taken up. The letters do not seem to have survived, but some of the characters were recalled when Louis wrote to Katharine in the autumn of 1886.

He had particularly enjoyed the Rev. Barwell Smith and a young man called Sneak, apparently on a mission to relieve the genteel well-to-do of their wealth and redistribute it among the poor of India. This, Louis suggested, might lead to a court case after Sneak was caught 'visiting houses with a subscription list and purloining articles from the hall tables'. At the home of one Mrs Anderson Watt, the court heard: 'The prisoner came to her house and cried about the natives of India; he was very soft spoken and she believed him. He seemed to feel the condition of the heathen acutely (laughter). She went upstairs to find a shilling, and when she came down he had gone away with a large umbrella, a greatcoat, a pair of pattens and a photograph album...'

Socialism was in its infancy and the two cousins might be forgiven their scepticism, although other literary figures took it seriously. Soon after the foundation of the Fabian Society in 1884, George Bernard Shaw would take up the cudgels on behalf of the deserving poor, addressing meetings up and down the country. The society's work appealed to freethinking intellectuals, from the designer William Morris and the early sexologist Havelock Ellis to bluestocking authors such as Edith Nesbit and Annie Besant, the latter estranged from her clergyman husband by her antipathy to religion and his tendency to pocket her earnings, as married women had no control over their own money. Yet while Mrs Besant's plight might seem similar to Katharine's, it was actually Sydney de Mattos who embraced socialism – and in the process a number of women involved in the movement. His estranged wife, now settled with their children at her mother's home in Chelsea, preferred to turn a blind eye to whatever 'distemperate and exorbitantly lecherous' view of life de Mattos might be pursuing within the Fabian Society.

She could always count on Bob, whose marriage to Louisa had not altered his close relationship with his sister. He was slowly making a name for himself as an art critic and he and Katharine encouraged each other's journalistic efforts. In the autumn of 1886 she had been commissioned to write a piece for the *Magazine of Art* about an artists' colony in France. Bob, unwilling to rekindle memories of Belle Osbourne at Grez, had taken refuge for a while at Cernay-la-Ville and it seems he introduced Katharine to the artists there. Among them was Louis's old friend Hiram Bloomer, who happily accepted a commission to illustrate the article. His sketches did not have to reflect a particular locale, as Katharine gave her colony the fictitious title of 'Sevray-sur-Vallais', and it made a charming piece for the December issue of the magazine:

## Apple-Tree Corner
By Katharine de Mattos

OUR determination to invade an artists' colony was no new thing, yet it was late in the year ere the purpose was accomplished, so late that the last apple and grape of Sevray-sur-Vallais were gathered and garnered, and ready to produce more exhilarating and definite results than the poetical roses and snows of yester years. Indeed, ere we departed, their effects, in the shape of early glasses of *vin doux* or cider, were already manifest in the deportment of the peasantry.

Our young relative the painter was waiting at the crossroads to disinter us from a most depressing diligence, and conduct us to the inn a few yards off. On the way there he tried to console us for the advanced season by the assurance that the mean, tufty little leaves still lingering on the twisted network of apple branches, were all-sufficient for serious art purposes. At dinner, too, more than one voice was heard rejoicing in the absence of the 'monotonous green tone' of full summer. An animated discussion, led by a dark man in a blue jersey, was the result of such an expression of views. He first inveighed gloomily against the limitations, dangers, and snares of certain greens, gathering as he proceeded as much fire and earnestness as the keenest disputant – the most perfervid splitter of hairs – on the obscurest theological topic might display. The uplifted finger beseeching a hearing, the eager gestures of warning, of reproof, and of counsel, suggested a discourse of absorbing and vital interest.

At a word the conversation suddenly turned into quite another channel, and dispelled the illusion. The chief characteristic, we found, of all their talk was the pleasant, desultory way it ran from one thing to another without the least warning. Most aspects of men and things, from the pure technicalities of the profession to the wildest speculations or confessions of faith on humanity, past, present, and to be, were discussed or touched upon. To help out argument, one illustration followed another, generally to the point, and usually expressed in the vivid slang of the studio. We had heard painters called 'conversationally limited', but the statement has since been looked upon as a fable. There were days when, after ample table-talk, and we were about to disperse, a further word, instead of proving final, only revealed fresh horizons, and we would mechanically relapse into our places, or linger about the room in fascinated attention or rejoinder.

It was not always so. Sometimes talk was scant and silence supreme, for of the common, the discomforting pressure that makes the weather or kindred topics appear more desirable than quiet there was none. Occasionally the very men who talked most would rush in to eat, and rush back again to work, so absorbed that thinking and feeding were done in silence; but this was rare.

We were not at all disposed to grumble at the strangely uncomfortable conditions of life inside the inn. Even the cruel access of cold which greeted us, and lingered for many days, making the whole place look 'unseasonable', chilled us physically only. With the painters themselves it was clearly a *parti pris* to ignore small discomforts, and praise everything that could be praised – at any rate, to 'outsiders' like ourselves. Some of the number we knew to be not quite ingenuous in their utter disregard and seeming unconsciousness of evils which, in another entourage, would have disturbed them. But here it all suited well with a certain 'painting attitude of mind'.

Sounds would come to us, on many a morning, of the north wind whistling ironically at rickety doors and windows, and frequent sluicings of cold water by the fat *femme du logis* over the already clammy brick flooring. The greater the outside damp, the more the good woman strove to encourage it within. Vast quantities of water were consumed in what seemed worse than useless labour, and sometimes little was to be had for better purposes. But when she swept or cleaned, as she too often did at ill-timed moments, no one murmured, not a voice was raised in unkindly criticism of her domestic economics. A friendly woman was this hostess of ours, perhaps not energetic in other departments, but throwing soul and body into voluble talk and water-pouring.

Sometimes she kept both going together, whilst her bearded guests stamped energetically about on the bricks to keep up their circulation, lowered by wandering for hours after motives, through sloppy lanes and field-paths.

In spite of weather, and as loth to leave them, many of the men retained hats, of strange shape and size, fitted to ward off tropical sunshine at the least. True, the radiance of St Martin's summer was still expected to vindicate their presence, with the help of their wearers' good looks; but, in the meantime, they flapped somewhat disconsolately over storm-ridden locks and reddened ears.

When that ephemeral season did arrive, we were as ready to enjoy it as the lazy, enthusiastic, talkative, dreamy people around us, so full of contradictions and anomalous qualities. Fond of the place – especially after a sunshiny hour or two – to the extent of disloyalty to all others, they even made light, and that with no dubious earnestness, of the *'taillis de Fontaine-bleau si' passionnément aimés des peintres'*, as Fromentin says somewhere. Thus is the real nature artiste constructed; and it does not fear to contradict itself, nor to change and waver a thousand times a day on the matter of likes and dislikes, and gaily to dismiss logical conclusions whenever they become troublesome.

Even without these litanies of praise we should have discovered that it was a pleasant and pretty little place, full of variety and interest. But we should never have found out for ourselves all the hidden beauties and subtle expressions in the scenery. Much was, indeed, worthy of the seeing eye and the understanding mind; and these remarkable features were continually reviewed. Our friends assured us they contained – within how small an area it would be impossible to say – every imaginable variety of scenery. There was 'a kind of sentiment about' that suggested the Low Countries; something else recalled the 'feeling' of the Alps or Apennines; elsewhere it was a district of Scotland or Southern Africa. The great waste places of oriental lands were also duly represented by vague indications in a lonely cabbage plantation that seemed to have 'gone wrong'. A demand (it is to be feared, a flippant one) for so specific an article as the Yosemite Valley proved the pioneers, and their country, equal to the occasion. If we did not get the Yosemite precisely, we were at any rate invited to inspect the 'idea' of it, to be obtained by noting certain relations between something and something else. What a field for an intelligent artist! What a sum of advantages condensed into one small corner of the universe! Even to an ordinary observer there was a marked variety on a miniature scale in the local characteristics which, under these favouring circumstances, developed enormously.

Sometimes we set forth to look at things in Biblical-like bands of disciples, listening to the discourse of one inspired person. Sometimes, for a spell, everybody talked at once; and, if nobody was benefited, none was the worse. Our way often led across the high levels: so often that the long stretches of ploughed land, dotted with the crooked and beloved apple-tree, became very familiar spectacles to us. We admired, at leisure, the purply warmth of the upturned earth, and the stout horses labouring. Aspects of sunset, sunrise, or broad afternoon, were described in technical terms by a group of enthusiasts breathing forth fresh notes of admiration at one's elbow, and appearing unable for weeks together, through overweening admiration and intelligent comprehension of the scene (or what to the unworthy sometimes appeared no scene), to register their impressions on canvas. It was cheering to know that so many fine conceptions and so much careful observation were at least immortalised in conversation.

Thus, pausing and sauntering, with earnest gesticulation, and sundry tarryings, that led to the loss of one or more of the party by the way, we would descend to the valley beneath. Here is the enchanted ground – the happy valley of painters. Here the light and air shift and change continually, there is an interminable dynasty of aspects; and the place never fails to suggest to them fresh intellectual or technical problems.

To the uninitiate it perhaps looks no more than a bit of woodland, but it is always bristling with camp-stools, easels, and figures, feverishly or meditatively at work. Every one found his material and worked it as he liked; the streamlet, with its dark rocks and trees, never twice wore the same aspect in nature or on canvas; vocal only with the wandering rivulet setting to tiny waterfalls or calm basins, and flooded all over with luminous darkness, half-tints, and mysterious glimmerings, the groves just then 'a pale, frail mist', the grey sky caught in meshes of crossed branches, it had a witchery of its own that infected one readily. Dawn and twilight visited it with hopeful or tender gleams, and in broad day, when everything else fainted under garish light and laughter, it held its own secret. Under a bright and breezy sky it took on a delicate and sylvan, almost a piquant, grace, dotted about with sudden notes of bright-hued, moving raiment, frail gossamers and airy flounces rustling through the trees; alive with the presence and voices of charming little persons who looked upon the tiny cascade and the miniature crags as difficulties insurmountable without the help of small cries and much encouragement. In all these phases, and a hundred more, it was the subject of innumerable notes, sketches, and studies. Even then it was not exhausted, for it haunted many a conversation. The next best thing to painting is, not to buy pictures, but to watch others paint, or to listen to intelligent talk on the subject. There was no lack of opportunity of the kind here.

One wholesome feature was the daily discussion of work and methods. The still wet canvases were brought to the *salle à manger* and ranged in the best light; the day's labours were criticised, encouraged, joked over, more to the profit than the hurt of any one concerned. The true story of the British artist, his lonely and secret pilgrimage in fear of his brethren, and in search of a picture, came back to one. Here no one called an embryo idea his own, certain that it must become so in due course.

The dinner hour was perhaps the pleasantest of the day; if 'shop' was banished it was not for long, and we forgot to be sorry when it recurred. The food was mediocre enough, though the hospitable hostess, handing and pressing her dishes, praised them and herself unreservedly. '*Regardez-moi ce petit M____*,' she would say, pointing to a guest, '*qui cligne, qui fait les petits yeux*; he knows what is good and what to expect of my cooking.' And he probably did, having long been detained, on parole, in the establishment.

The total eclipse and disappearance of debtors in their simple working attire of blouse and sabots, untrammelled by aught save a pochade box and the bare means of reaching Paris, is perhaps a more characteristic feature of these resorts. Payments by instalments from distant creditors brimming over with good intentions and small results were so rare as to excite a feeling more akin to bewildered amusement than satisfaction in the recipients. If a kindly faith in his ultimate success can help a man whilst his bill is acquiring a dreadful length – is running on, as the wit said, as if it would never stop – the sanguine host and hostess were helping more than one along the thorny path to fame and fortune.

By evening the train of a long-laid fire was fairly ablaze – that kind of fire that might roast an ox, but only served to roast the humbler chestnut accompanied by white wine, when, dinner over, we gathered round the wide chimney. On some nights the lurid fires of Paris were said to redden the horizon; but we sat round our own hearth, and the restless centre, so near us, seemed far enough away. 'Tis true, some one would occasionally take a plunge and disappear there for a few days, returning, less with the wrecked aspect of the traditional pleasure-seeker, than overflowing with fresh news and interests.

The piano was often in use to cheer us; but otherwise the furniture was scanty, and the room bare – bare, that is, if a room can be called bare whose walls are alive with fancies, and where there is not a bit of blank space to stare one stupidly in the face. For, as at Barbizon and Grez, as at most artist haunts, these walls are crowded with memories. Hands of the great dead and the living have set their seal on these walls and turned them into a rich phantasmagoria of suggestions, visions, real sights, and dream scenes of all sorts. The signatures of Corot and of Français, the pathetic name of Heraut and the robust touch of Pelouse (and how many more!), are all to be found there. Perhaps the sight reacts on the spectators, and helps to accentuate the rambling, brilliant, and imaginative character of their talk. Certain it is, these 'pictured places' give rise to many a story, grave or gay, to much poignant discussion, to unuttered thoughts and aspirations, that may have helped many a man to paint – perhaps to live.

* *

Life went on for Katharine and Bob, despite her losing her childhood love to Fanny and his failure to win the love of Fanny's daughter. Belle was now living with her artist husband and their young son Austin in Hawaii. There Joe's talents as a painter had won him the patronage of King David Kalakaua, a legendary drinker who knocked back champagne like water. The Strongs moved in the best Hawaiian society but Joe could not handle the drink and like poor Walter Ferrier became a hopeless alcoholic.

Back in Britain, Belle's brother lived a life of privilege as Louis's much-indulged stepson, attending Edinburgh University but dropping out with eye problems which seemed curiously to resolve themselves with the aid of spectacles once he had been sent off on a long holiday to the West Indies. Samuel Lloyd was still out of the country when shocking news came from California, just before his 19th birthday. On 28 March 1887, Sam Osbourne had vanished. Belle learned that her father had gone to the courthouse for a night session, asking his second wife to have supper for him at midnight. He kissed her, and went off down the street whistling. Later he left the court house a little before midnight, in his usual good spirits... and disappeared, his passing marked only by a pile of clothes discovered later on a beach.

It seemed Fanny's first husband had been no more inclined than Sydney de Mattos to give up his philandering. Following the divorce, Osbourne had married an unfortunate woman called Rebecca Paul, known as 'Pauly', but had not relinquished his wayward lifestyle. On hearing the news of his disappearance, Fanny wrote: 'The papers say there are "evil rumours" concerning him, one being that he has deserted his miserable wife and fled with a young girl employed in his office.'

As the wife of a popular children's author, Fanny was acutely aware that the disreputable disappearance of her former husband could be not only embarrassing for her and her family but commercially damaging to Louis. The scandal might even rub off on young Sam, who from then on used only his middle name Lloyd and tried to forget the father he once idolised. His mother was still on tenterhooks – 'I am so afraid of the past' – when news from Edinburgh put their troubles in perspective. Louis's father was very ill and sinking fast.

Tom Stevenson had been slowly losing a battle with dementia that plunged him into Calvinistic gloom. Louis, despite his own ill health, had taken his father a few months previously to the Derbyshire spa town of Matlock in a bid to lift his spirits. As Mr Stevenson's mind deteriorated, his personality could be gentle and childlike, then suddenly transformed by the rage of old age. From Smedley's Hydropathic Hotel, Louis wrote to his mother: 'My father, I am sorry to say, gave me a full dose of Hyde this morning. He began about breakfast as usual; and then to prove himself in the right and that he did well to be angry, carried on a long time (obviously on purpose) about the moon. I was very severe with him, and refused to speak again till he was quiet; after which he admitted he had been very silly...'

Now the old man's life was drawing to a close. Louis and Fanny at once set off by train for Edinburgh, arriving to find Tom Stevenson still alive but oblivious to his surroundings. Katharine had heard the news and had written at once to Heriot Row. Louis replied to her mother's home in Chelsea: 'Katharine's kind letter reached me here this morning and tells me you are so far prepared. I can only say that when I came yesterday he could not be made to recognise me. He suffers not at all, is really unconscious; yet he ate some luncheon yesterday, and the day before smoked a cigarette...'

The following day, Mr Stevenson died. Louis was now so ill that he could not attend the funeral, but Katharine's brother Bob had come north and stood in for him at the biggest private ceremony Edinburgh had seen. Eventually Louis recovered enough to speak to the family solicitor about his father's will, which left everything to his mother but with the proviso that Bob and Katharine should be taken care of – discharging a duty of care to the children of 'poor Alan'. From then on Louis was in the awkward position of paying both his cousins an allowance.

He and Fanny returned to Bournemouth, where Louis's health continued to be a worry. He was no longer tied to the British Isles by the need to be near his ailing father, while his 58-year-old mother was showing great strength of character in coping with bereavement. When her son told her he needed to go abroad but would not countenance leaving without her, she agreed to accompany her 'darling Lou' with Fanny and Lloyd to America.

Arrangements were made to shut up Skerryvore, and a passage was booked to New York. The sudden departure came as a shock to Louis's many literary friends, who feared that in leaving cultured England for the brashness of the States he was committing professional suicide. While waiting to board the cargo vessel Ludgate Hill for the transatlantic journey, the Stevensons stayed at a hotel in London's Finsbury where friends and relatives called to say goodbye. Katharine came, along with Coggie Ferrier, both women well aware of how serious Louis's illness could be, and how his life hung always on a thread. During the tearful farewells, Katharine probably knew in her heart of hearts that she and the cousin she had loved for so long would never see each other again.

# 9

# The Stolen Story

'IF JESUS CHRIST came, they would make less fuss.' Looking down on the sea of upturned faces on the quayside in New York, Louis was learning what it meant to be a celebrity. He had scarcely left the ship when he was mobbed by reporters, eager to interview the famous author. It seemed the whole city had gone *Jekyll and Hyde* crazy. Already the expression had entered the language as shorthand for a dual personality – even the pilot who had seen the Ludgate Hill safely into port had been nicknamed 'Mr Hyde' by his crew, with his more easygoing second-in-command dubbed 'Dr Jekyll'.

In the wake of the reporters came the magazine proprietors, eager to sign up Louis as a star contributor. He turned down the astronomical sum of £2,000 for a year's worth of weekly articles, on the grounds that his health could never stand it, but accepted £600 for a dozen articles in *Scribner's Magazine*. Back in London, Henley was astonished by his friend's wealth and fame and hoped it might help his own prospects.

An attempt by Louis to get some of Henley's poetry accepted by *Scribner's* had met with a polite refusal, but a production of Deacon Brodie was now touring the States, staged by a theatre company run by Henley's ne'er-do-well actor brother Teddy. Yet despite Teddy's claims of success, the play written by Henley and Louis did badly everywhere except Chicago, while performances were cancelled after an unseemly drunken punch-up involving Teddy and his actors in a Philadelphia bar. Unabashed, Teddy then asked Louis for money to keep the show on the road, and was displeased when all Louis would offer him was his fare back home to England. For Henley, the play's failure and his brother's disgraceful behaviour came as a heavy double blow.

Meanwhile Louis was delighted to learn his own first volume of poetry, entitled Underwoods and published four days after he left England, was already selling well. Katharine would have been pleased to see it contained two poems dedicated to her, the first harking back to their childhood. Although written at Hyères in 1883, when Katharine was a struggling single mother, it recalls the fey teenage girl with whom young Louis had been smitten as they roamed the Borders countryside or perhaps lay together on a bed of wild blueberries, reading the exploits of Dick Turpin.

### To K. De M.

A lover of the moorland bare
And honest country winds, you were;
The silver-skimming rain you took;
And loved the floodings of the brook,
Dew, frost and mountains, fire and seas,
Tumultuary silences,
Winds that in darkness fifed a tune,
And the high-riding, virgin moon.

And as the berry, pale and sharp,
Springs on some ditch's counterscarp
In our ungenial, native north –
You put your frosted wildings forth,
And on the heath, afar from man,
A strong and bitter virgin ran.

The berry ripened keeps the rude
And racy flavour of the wood.
And you that loved the empty plain
All redolent of wind and rain,
Around you still the curlew sings –
The freshness of the weather clings –
The maiden jewels of the rain
Sit in your dabbled locks again.

How would Katharine feel now about the cousin she adored recalling her as a 'strong and bitter virgin', sharp as a blueberry? His second poem about her, originally penned as an afterthought in the margin of the first, was perhaps kinder, portraying her as a sort of elfin watersprite – curiously anticipating the subject of her unsellable short story.

### Katharine

We see you as we see a face
That trembles in a forest place
Upon the mirror of a pool
Forever quiet; clear and cool;

And in the wayward glass, appears
To hover between smiles and tears,
Elfin and human, airy and true,
And backed by the reflected blue.

When Katharine's copy of *Underwoods* dropped through the letterbox in St Leonard's Terrace, Louis and Fanny were staying as guests of the Boston investment banker Charles Fairchild and his wife Elizabeth at their summer home in Newport, Rhode Island. The Fairchilds were delighted to have the famous author staying with them and Mr Fairchild commissioned a portrait of Louis by the society painter John Singer Sargent.

For Louis, the Fairchilds' wealth provided ten days of seclusion from the adoring public while he and Fanny found themselves a new home in Saranac Lake, New York State. There Dr Edward Livingston Trudeau, a world expert on tuberculosis, ran a sanatorium. The Stevensons moved into a small wooden house nearby and prepared for a bitter winter, equipping themselves with heavy coats made from buffalo hide. The intense cold and clear air were meant to be good for Louis's delicate lungs, and Trudeau provided the best of care, although his tests revealed no active tuberculosis. In these strange surroundings, Louis began work on his next novel, *The Master of Ballantrae*, along with his monthly contributions to *Scribner's Magazine*.

Saranac Lake was emerging from winter temperatures colder than 20 below zero when the March 1988 issue of *Scribner's* hit the newsstands. In it was a charming piece entitled '*Beggars*', by Robert Louis Stevenson. When Henley opened his copy of *Scribner's* in London, he was keen to read what his friend had written for £50 – a common labourer's wages for a year. As always, the RLS style was in evidence as Louis reflected on the begging trade, the stories spun by beggars and the blessings heaped on his head in return for his small change: 'Everyone lives by selling something, whatever be his right to it. The burglar sells at the same time his own skill and courage and my silver plate... The bandit sells the traveller an article of prime necessity: that traveller's life...' There were no genuine beggars, Louis opined: 'The true poverty does not go into the streets; the banker may rest assured, he has never put a penny in its hand. The self-respecting poor beg from each other; never from the rich...'

While this would have delighted Louis's growing readership, it would not impress Henley. Unlike Louis, who had never needed to beg for anything, Henley knew what it was like to depend on the charity of others, entreating Joseph Lister to admit him to the Edinburgh Infirmary and save his leg. Henley had quite cheerfully accepted loans and gifts of money from Louis, without so much as a 'God bless you, kind gentleman', but he had also given unsparingly of his time and energy promoting his friend's work and securing publishing deals without taking a fee. Now it seemed Long John Silver's help was no longer necessary, with the gold falling effortlessly into Louis's lap. Yet while Henley could not help being depressed by his own circumstances since being forced out of the editorship of the *Magazine of Art*, he genuinely wished his friend well. If Louis could make a fortune writing about beggars, more power to his elbow.

Then Henley turned to another piece in the same issue of Scribner's, advertised as the work of 'Mrs Robert Louis Stevenson'. He could forgive Fanny for trading on her husband's name to get into print – but his jaw dropped when he saw the story that had been the source of so much frustration for Katharine and himself:

## The Nixie
### By Fanny Van de Grift Stevenson

SNUGLY ensconced in one corner of a first-class railway carriage, an athletic, good-looking young man stretched his long limbs lazily, half opened his eyes, closed them again, yawned mightily, and then sank back into luxurious slumber. He had entered the carriage from a country station, equipped with a trout-basket and fishing-tackle, and was evidently bent on whipping the streams which wound among the neighbouring hills. It was very early, and raw and cold with the chill of an English morning. Willoughby, having tipped the guard generously, and his destination being yet some three-quarters of an hour distant, shut his eyes with the comfortable assurance that he might finish his morning's nap in peace. He had scarcely, however, floated away into that delectable land of 'negative gravity' when he was startled into sudden wakefulness by an animal-like shriek of terror so close at hand that it tingled in his ears. The train was passing through a tunnel, and, as often happened at that early hour, the lamp in the roof had been neglected, and the carriage was filled with smoke and darkness; the tunnel was long, but at last a glimmer of light began to penetrate the gloom. It was with a glow of anger against the corruptibility of the guard he had himself bribed, that Willoughby discerned the outlines of a small figure crouched in the opposite bench; a child, he had at first thought, which accounted for the quality of the shriek;

and then, with increasing annoyance, a schoolgirl. Willoughby turned over in his mind the terms of his coming interview with the faithless guard. His privacy, for which he had paid liberally, had been violated, and his comfort destroyed. Sleep, so rudely assaulted, had fled his eyes. He leaned back and gazed sullenly out of the window at the coming day, alas too fair, too clear, belying the promise of a hunting morning.

The sun rose higher, and soon flooded the windows with dazzling light. The young man drew down the blinds, and turned his disapproving gaze upon the pitiful intruder. He wondered idly, as she shrank before him, what mistaken chance had led her into a first-class carriage, from which she must certainly be ousted at the first stoppage, every detail of her appearance being so frankly suggestive of that station in society for the members of which third-class carriages are specially designed. The new, blue cotton gown of ungainly cut, with straight short sleeves; the large, coarse boots, hardly soiled as yet with use; the stiff straw hat scantily trimmed with a mean red ribbon – the hat not a fit, the gown not a fit, the shoes not a fit – marked the girl unmistakeably as the recent recruit of some charitable or reformatory institution. To arrive at an explanation of her stealthy entrance and incongruous position, was not difficult; the girl was a runaway. A second glance at her face corroborated the silent confession of her attire. The small dark eyes, darting hither and thither, were scouting for danger, and had the expression of a wood animal troubled with the vague suspicion of instinct at a loss. The shapeless gown hinted here and there of delicately turned contours, but also of the angularities of early girlhood, and possibly of privation and ill-treatment.

Willoughby was young, and the sympathy of youth with rebellion some-what softened his heart towards the fugitive – fleeing, perhaps, from good to evil; but a fugitive. At every unusual sound or movement, the girl shrank and quivered, recalling to the young man's memory an incident of his boyhood. Once, in his schooldays, when he was hiding in the branches of a tree with an interdicted novel, a hare, hard pressed by the hounds, took refuge in the grass beneath him. Her repressed starts of terror, her wild dilated eyes filled him with pity. But what a hypocrite and time-server is the boy; though he could not betray the hunted thing, when the dogs, followed by the sportsmen, closed in upon her, he shut his eyes with a sick heart, and joined with the others in their loud acclamation.

These reminiscences, and some pointed reflections that were passing through Willoughby's mind, were cut short by the slowing of the train to a station. On the impulse of the moment, he stepped to the door, squaring his shoulders, and spreading his arm as a shield to screen the interior of the carriage. To give countenance to the scrutiny of possible pursuers, he called an old woman carrying an armful of water lilies, and chaffered for her wares until the train was again in motion. 'What a silly unkindness is the kindness of the sentimentalist,' he thought, as he threw the moist flowers on the seat beside him; 'because I once saw a hare caught by hounds, I aid and abet a workhouse brat to escape from her safest friends; and to what end? Her destination can but be, after an aimless round, the shelter whence she came; or failing that, destruction.' He turned to his fellow traveller.

'Well, my good girl,' he began, in the condescending tone of the moralist, 'Where are you bound for?'

'I don't know,' was the answer he received and expected.

'Why did you run away?'

The girl, who had been casting furtive glances at the bunch of lilies, frowned, then smiled with an expression that startled him with a curious sense of familiarity, and plucking first at the breast of her gown, knocked upon the top of her hard head gear. Frowning again, she suddenly straightened her legs, bringing the heavy leathern boots on a level with Willoughby's knees.

'At least that is better than going barefoot, or having no clothes at all,' replied the young man to her pantomimic protest. 'I fear you are an ungrateful _____'

A wave of terror swept over the girl's face. 'Let me go! Let me go!' she cried, leaping to the opposite window. As Willoughby dragged her back, for in another moment she would have broken the glass and cut her hands, she beat at him savagely. She did not repeat her attempt to escape, but cowered on the seat where he dropped her, regarding him with the stare of a cat at bay.

'I don't wonder,' thought Willoughby, 'that the death of the hare sticks in my throat, for I feel like a hound. The girl is honestly running away, while I, who presume to lecture her, am fleeing in a sham, half-hearted way, to sneak back, after my few hours of stolen freedom, like a cur with my tail between my legs, to a round of conventions as galling to me as the penitentiary rules are to her.'

With a changed voice and manner, he now addressed himself to the task of soothing the girl. As his advances were received with quick alarm, he fell back on his boyish experiences as a trapper, and simulated sleep, watching, meanwhile, the effect through his lashes. The girl gradually ceased panting, and the lurking terror in her eyes gave place to a sly intelligence. For a long time she remained perfectly quiet. Willoughby, tired of his constrained attitude, was about to speak, when she made an abrupt movement, evidently to test the genuineness of his slumber. Once more she made the experiment, and then, to the young man's dismay, darted forth a swift hand, detached one of the lilies, hid it the folds of her gown, and relapsed into quietude. Willoughby was surprised at the shock this gave him. He knew, now, that the flitting resemblance to an intangible image that he could not lay hold of, had been playing odd tricks in some remote corner of his brain, and that he was unconsciously fitting this charity stray upon a pedestal, and arranging her young limbs in a classic pose. With the annoyance one feels at losing a word, or the continuity of a thought however trivial, he racked his mind for the clue which was playing hide and seek with his memory.

But these fruitless excursions into cul-de-sacs of the past were abruptly checked. It had been a long run since the last station, and Willoughby found himself at the end of his journey. He was taken unawares, and had no plans. That the girl must come to grief sooner or later, he felt sure, but a coin or two might postpone the evil moment. He hastily gathered his 'traps', and tossed into her lap several half-crowns; as they left his hand he saw that he had accidentally included a sovereign with the silver. Gold could only be a questionable and dangerous possession for the girl, and yet an unaccountable shamefacedness prevented his reclaiming it. As a last thought he laid upon her knees the bunch of lilies, which according to all rules, should have been as coals of fire on her head. She accepted them, however, without a blush, and instead of thanking him, lifted the corner of her skirt to show the pilfered flower, smiling in Willoughby's face with a mingled slyness, and frankness, and shyness that again sent his memory flying on a barren quest.

The young man walked musingly a few paces, paused irresolutely, almost with the intention of returning, but the whistle of the engine, and moving wheels decided the question. He had given up his ticket and passed through the gate, when his attention was arrested by the sound of a gruff voice saying,

'Now you come here! None of that, you know. You must give up your ticket.' A hand clasped his. The girl had followed him from the train, and now stood, apparently waiting for his decision with the doubtful confidence of a dog uncertain of its master's intentions. The money he had thrown her lay scattered on the ground, but the lilies she held to her breast.

Willoughby, feeling the position a little ridiculous, for the girl, now she stood beside him, was taller and older than he had supposed, gently loosened his hand, and addressed the gatekeeper in a conciliatory tone.

'I think,' said he, 'She has lost her ticket; but you see she has money,' picking it up and offering it as he spoke. The man touched his cap, named the fare, pocketed a little more with a 'thank you, sir,' and 'I suppose she's a little?' tapping his forehead significantly.

'It seems so,' said the young man, shifting his fishing implements about uneasily; 'Look here; take this, and see that she has a ticket on the return train, and look after her, like a good fellow, when it comes.'

The leering curiosity of the rustics who hang about the station brought a flush to his cheeks, and he turned with an angry stride towards a green lane which led, as he knew, through thick-growing beeches, skirted a field or two, and finally lost itself in a bit of forest land traversed by one fairly broad, and several narrower streams. The former he meant to follow back to its tributaries in the hills, where the trout cooled their sides in many shadowy pools dear to the fisher's heart. The morning fragrance of grasses, and blossoming weeds, and growing corn, and the exuding gums of trees, rose balmily as with the breath of waking day, and the joy of living thrilled in the air. Willoughby sniffed with expanded nostrils like a young horse, and fell into the long, easy stride of the practiced walker. The girl gave him a few moments' vantage, watching apprehensively over one shoulder and the other, and then, hampered in her movements by the clumsy boots, and the folds of her gown, plodded heavily in his rear.

Willoughby, who was whistling softly to himself, mounted a stile that lay in his way, and from the top turned and looked out over the fair landscape. The figure of the girl, painfully trudging toward him, instantly caught his eye. With an impatient gesture, he sat down and waited for her to overtake him. As she came nearer, he noted with surprise the glow of colour that was on her cheeks and lips. The spirit of the morning that had quickened his pulses, had moved even the dull current in the veins of the workhouse waif. Willoughby found something pathetic in the thought. He gave her his hand, and helped her over the stile, checking his steps involuntarily to her limit. He fell into a confused reverie. Before his mind's eye rose a vision of his father's house, now filled with summer visitors; ladies, with their bazaars, their tennis, their 'work,' and their flirting; dull, urbane old gentlemen; dull young gentlemen whose sullen hearts were gnawed by tedium. In Willoughby's distorted imagination these really estimable persons revolved stupidly, like the spokes of a wheel, round a common centre, Lady Maud Ponsonby. He knew that Lady Maud was his destined bride; she knew it, and their respective parents knew it, though no word had been spoken. It seemed more that it must be, because there was absolutely no reason why it should not be. These meditations, which had somewhat damped the buoyancy of his spirits, were interrupted by a pluck at his sleeve.

'There is a river yonder,' said the girl, pointing across the fields; 'A river.'

'How came you to be taken to the – the institution?' asked Willoughby, irrelevantly, with a start.

'They caught me in a trap, and shut me up, and put these upon me,' was the indignant reply, 'But they shall not do that again; they cannot catch me now. They catch birds, too,' she added; 'I cannot understand it; can you?'

'I suppose I can,' answered Willoughby. 'Look there, at yonder thieving rascal, how he is pecking away at the grapes.'

They were passing the end of a walled garden. A gate stood open, and just inside, a hothouse door swung on its hinges. A blackbird, taking advantage of the gardener's negligence, was busy at the amber fruit. In a moment the girl was beside him, adding a couple of bunches and a handful of vine leaves to the lilies she still carried. The bird chirped angrily, but did not move.

'I cannot allow this,' said Willoughby; 'Take back those grapes, and shut the door.'

'No,' said the girl; 'I want them, so why should I put them back?'

'You know very well, they are not yours to take.'

'Not mine? But you saw me gather them!'

'You know that they belong to the man who planted the roots, and built the glass house,' persisted Willoughby, irritated at having this primitive lesson in morality forced from him. Had it been the escapade of a young lady, he knew he should have joined, and found it great sport; but the thought of the workhouse made preaching incumbent on him.

'No, they are not his,' said the girl; 'The man did not make the root; he could not. And the sun, and the air, and the rain, made the fruit grow upon it. The man shut the root in a prison, and now you say he claims its children. I do not understand that.'

'If you think you are justified in helping yourself to whatever you may fancy,' asked Willoughby, 'Why then did you not openly take the lily when we were in the train?'

'Everybody knows,' replied the girl, 'That there are many dangerous things abroad. A snake under a strawberry plant may not want to eat the berry, but if you do, you must be very cautious in gathering it, or he may strike you. Then the large and more terrible creatures who are greedy like the blackbird, and wish to keep more than they need – with them, one must be wary indeed! I thought you were one of those at first.'

'Oh,' remarked Willoughby.

'Yes; I was afraid of you, then. I am not, now. You did not really care for my taking the grapes, you only feared someone might see me, and I should be caught in your company.'

The girl's unexpected shrewdness of observation, the absence of vulgarity in her speech or manner, coupled with her reformatory dress, began to puzzle Willoughby exceedingly. 'Where have you lived all your life?' he asked abruptly.

'There,' was the answer, with a wave of the hand that swept half the horizon. There was not much information to be derived from a statement so comprehensive.

Willoughby tried again. 'How old are you?'

'Oh – a hundred – a hundred thousand days. And you, how old are you?'

'Just turned my 23rd year,' answered Willoughby, shortly.

'I shouldn't have thought you were so old.'

'I suppose, then, I must look younger than I am,' said he, not quite pleased that he had given so strong an impression of youth.

'On the contrary, you look very, very old,' said the girl; but this assertion was still less to Willoughby's taste.

By the time they reached the forest belt the sun was high, and Willoughby, feeling the fatigue of walking at a pace so much slower than his custom, would have stopped to rest, but the girl pushed on eagerly to the river. Here, Willoughby leaned his rod against a tree, and disembarrassed himself of his trout-basket, which at present contained a packet of sandwiches, and a half bottle of claret. Having arranged these matters to his satisfaction, he turned to resume his conversation with the girl, whose quaint remarks and savage ignorance of the ordinary convenances of life, he was beginning, in spite of himself, to find both interesting and amusing. To his amazement, she was apparently disrobing herself. Her hat lay upon the ground, with the ribbon that had bound her hair into a pigtail beside it. The bodice of her gown she was in the act of removing; holding it up, she laughed derisively, and tossed it far out into some brambles.

'Come,' she said, beckoning to Willoughby; 'We must take care of the lilies first. Gathering them together, she laid several in the crown of the hard hat that had left a mark across her brow, ballasted the hat with pebbles, and sent it floating down the stream. The coarse shoes, one after the other, their respective stockings in their toes, and freighted with lilies, followed the hat.

'I say,' cried Willoughby, 'You had better stop there! People *do* come this way.'

In another second his own 'deerstalker' was seized, weighted, filled with the remaining lily pods, and this frail shallop joined the argosy. Shaking the drops from her hair, which had trailed in the water, the girl rose and turned towards the young man.

'Do not look so strangely,' she said; 'They may not live long, but they shall at least die at home.'

'Who are you?' cried Willoughby, passing his hand across his eyes. 'Who are you?'

'Come,' she said; 'Come and eat, you are tired.'

She laid the stolen grapes on a flat stone, and began to fold a vine leaf into the form of a cup. Willoughby, at her bidding, spread his contribution to the feast beside the grapes. The girl raised a warning finger, filled her green cup at the stream, deliberately spilled a portion, murmuring a few inaudible words, and offered the rest to Willoughby.

'Is it – is it a – *libation*?' he asked, incredulously.

'It is,' she answered; 'And now eat and drink, and rest.'

A short time before, Willoughby would not have hesitated to offer the girl stumbling at his side a sip of gin from the mouth of a square bottle; but since she had cast off the clumping boots, and the pinching, dragging bodice of her gown, she moved with an alert grace that even Lady Maud might have envied. The world over, it is the same; beauty in the female develops chivalry in the male. And now Willoughby was abashed by the difficulty of dispensing his wine gracefully. The cork was already loosened; he drew it with his penknife, awkwardly filled the sylvan cup, and offered it to the girl, who had been watching his proceedings with uneasy curiosity. She touched the brim with shrinking lip.

'You have given me blood to drink!' she gasped.

Willoughby snatched the leaf from her hand, and, so strong is the sympathy of imagination, fancied that he, too, tasted blood in the cup. The meal was finished in silence, Willoughby swallowing his sandwiches with an uncomfortable sense of grossness, while the girl fed daintily on grapes. They drank clear water alternately from the same vine leaf, and even Willoughby, who was accounted to have a delicate palate for wine, and had accompanied the butler to the cellar that very morning to make sure of his favourite vintage, began to regard the bottle that stood between them with aversion.

'Let us bury it,' suggested the girl.

So they made a hole in the soft ground, digging with the joints of Willoughby's most tenderly cherished rod; and there an excellent half bottle of *La Rose* doubtless lies to-day. As they patted and shaped the tiny grave, the young man's thoughts wandered back to the morning, when, suave and cynically self-possessed, he drank a cup of tea in the grey semi-darkness with Lady Maud, complimenting that placid maiden on her heroism in joining him at such an unconceivable hour, and declaring himself her true knight. She had playfully invested him with the order of the red rose; the rose, once reposing on Lady Maud's chaste breast, was – oh, here, in his trousers pocket, sadly crushed and withered. What, Willoughby wondered, would be Lady Maud's sensations could she behold him now, engaged with all the seriousness of life and death in a child's game, his playfellow, whom he more than suspected to be mad, a half-naked girl just escaped from a reformatory?

The crumbs and grapes, the remains of the repast, together with the leafy cup, were left on the stone for the regalement of birds and passing travellers.

'One should never destroy,' said the girl, 'What another may use after him. Yonder, round the turn of the stream, is a boat; the man who made it did not break it up when his day's pleasure was over, but covered it and tied it fast for the next comer.'

Willoughby, while he doubted the disinterestedness of the builder's motives, did not question the girl's knowledge of the boat, and in the face of his late platitudes on the subject of theft (which he blushed to remember) proposed to take piratical possession of the craft, and row up the river. The girl, reversing their parts, gave him her hand, and they ran laughing along the green banks like two children. As they went further up the stream the features of the landscape changed. The trees grew larger, and in more isolated groups, with open stretches of meadow between them. Breathless with laughter and running, the pair stopped to rest under the shade of a great oak. By this time it was high noon, and the sun was beating straightly down.

'Wait here,' said the girl. She came lightly springing back, carrying sprays of broad-leaved water-weeds. Her hair twined about her in dripping tendrils; the coarse chemise, the charity skirt, fresh from the river, clung in wet folds round her slim young body like antique drapery.

'I remember – I remember,' cried Willoughby, starting up. She signed him to stoop, but he knelt at her feet instead, while she bound the leaves in a wreath about his head.

'There,' she said, studying the effect with satisfaction; 'That is much better; that other must have been old and dry from the first.'

Willoughby had a moment's difficulty in understanding this remark, which gave him a sudden distaste, not only for the lost 'deerstalker,' now on its way to sodden destruction, but for his entire wardrobe. The dull blue of the girl's skirt, the unbleached linen of her chemise, harmonised with the tints of tree, and grass, and sky. The young man's correct bilious brown suit became hideous by comparison. No plunge into the river could mould those odious 'bags,' or the belted jacket, into classic lines. He was saved from heaven knows what folly by the voice of the girl calling him to follow her. *Follow – follow –* her words came echoing back from the opposite shore.

'*Hark!*' cried Willoughby.

The girl, checked in the very movement of running, slowly raised her hand to her ear, and stood silent as a statue. Hark! returned the echo. But it was not to that she was listening. Her head was turned over her shoulder, away from the river, and towards the wood. Willoughby listened intently. The light air moving among leaves, and across lithe twigs, made, now and then, a small, whistling, singing sound, the shadow of a strain as it were, so that he could almost persuade himself that he heard something like a distant, jocund piping.

'Is it the great god Pan?' he asked, softly. His voice broke the spell. The girl started and laid a finger on her lips. Coarse and mundane noises disturbed the musical silence. The loud laughter and chattering of approaching strangers sounded close at hand. Willoughby's first impulse was to secure the boat, which lay nearby. He leaped into the stern, unfastened the rope, and pushed a foot or two from the shore. Another boat, awkwardly handled by a couple of Cockney lads and their sweethearts, was coming down the stream. He cast an anxious look about him, but he was apparently alone. The occupants of the boat, flushed, and blowsy, and happy, regarded him with amazement. 'Oh,' cried one, 'He must be crazy! He's got a wreath on his head like the mad woman in the play. Perhaps he's a dangerous lunatic; oh, let us get away!' The young men bent to their oars, the boat lurched round the bend of the river and disappeared amid much splashing and giggling.

The incident jarred on Willoughby's mood. He waited several minutes, gazing abstractedly over the side of the boat, before calling to his companion. What was it, he wondered, that gave him such a new and vivid sense of kinship with the earth, so that he seemed to feel within himself its very essence and component parts? Had something got into his blood, something wild and natural, something with a tang like the sap of trees, and cool, and fresh, like the water of the river? He should scarcely have been surprised had his feet struck root in the ground, or leaves sprouted from his fingertips. He laughed aloud for simple joyousness when he saw the girl's reflection beside his own. A passing ripple shook the surface of the water, disturbing the mirrored face; the chin and lips quivered, the eyes became blurred, and the picture shattered into a thousand sparkles.

'It is an evil omen,' said the girl from over his shoulder. 'Let us go far up the river, and never, never return here again.'

'Never,' repeated Willoughby, absently. 'There are pools, and waterfalls, and glens up there,' continued the girl, 'and no hateful creatures to frighten us. How brave you are! You were not afraid; while I – I am trembling – make haste; make haste!'

Willoughby seized the oars and sent the boat out into the middle of the stream. The river ran merrily past them; birds sang in the trees that fringed the banks; the balmy summer air fanned their cheeks with the fragrance of a thousand flowers. Surely it was an enchanted boat carrying them into an enchanted land. Willoughby's sensations became strangely confused; he felt like a man in a dream; a humming was in his ears, and the images before his eyes danced, and changed in hue and form. It caused him no astonishment that the oars became light as thistledown, and he seemed to be grasping slippery, moist stalks, while the girl, her hands upon the stern, her feet floating out behind her, pushed the boat smoothly against the current, with eyes shining like glow-worms, and her lips parted in elfish glee. Nor was he surprised when the shyest of woodland birds perched upon his shoulders, or prize trout leaped beside the craftiest angler in England. His voice sounded faint, and sweet, and distant, as though someone else were speaking, as he dreamily recounted ancient tales, mixing naiads, and gods, and water-sprites into a romantic story of the present, where the principal characters were borne by himself and the girl.

It might have been a year, it might have been a day that passed. Shadows thickened, and a cold mist began to creep over the ground. Wild fowl whirred above their nests, calling their broods with plaintive cries. All about there was a scuttling and rustling of birds and beasts hurrying to their precarious homes in tree or earth. Willoughby shivered; the tale turned into unmeaning words on his lips; a weight bore upon his breast, and his head swam. Was his dream turning into a nightmare? The boat rocked; swaying dizzily over its side, he looked straight down into a face that sank deeper and deeper, the smile upon it changing grotesquely through the water from gay mockery to the grieved expression of a sobbing child, until it was lost in blackness.

Willoughby uttered an exclamation of horror. The girl was drowning before his eyes! He leaped after her, and dived again and again, until he was helpless from exhaustion, and cramped by the cold. The boat, meanwhile, half-filled with water, drifted heavily away.

When Willoughby recovered consciousness, he found himself lying on the grass, supported against the knee of a stranger, and surrounded by a group of young people whose vulgar faces he vaguely recognised. He tried to speak, but his lips moved without words.

'You are not strong enough yet, wait a little,' said a kind voice. 'You wonder what has happened, and where you are, I don't doubt. These young men told my gardener that they had seen you with my favourite boat. We came up here to look after my property, and found you instead, and pulled you out of the water where you had been upset, just in the nick of time – what is it? "Save the girl," he says. Was there a girl with him?'

'No, sir,' replied a Cockney voice. 'He was quite alone. He was standing in the boat with a wreath on his head, looking very dangerous, indeed, sir, and it's my belief that it's a sunstroke. I've looked in his pockets, as you directed, sir, and I can't find no card, nor nothing, only this messy old flower.'

# 10

# Cousin Hyde

HENLEY READ '*THE NIXIE*' with a growing sense of anger. Admittedly Fanny's direct way with words, from which Louis had no doubt removed all rough edges, gave the story the commercial appeal Katharine's original lacked, but that was not the point. It was Katharine's story and anyone with eyes in their head could have seen she never wanted to surrender it, however many times it had been rejected. To Henley's strong, natural sense of justice it seemed monstrously unfair that some people had to struggle for every hard-won ounce of success while others seemed to achieve it so easily – even by stealing an idea from a friend. He would have to say something to Louis.

Yet as Henley sat down to write to his friend from unfashionable but cheap Chiswick, to which he and Anna had recently moved, he had other things to confide that caused him unusually to mark the letter 'Private and Confidential'. The hospitalised young poet whose head had once been 'bloody but unbowed' was now approaching middle age, in constant pain from his remaining leg and experiencing black despair.

He began with all the old Long John Silver swagger, ribbing his friend for being saddled with domestic chores after Fanny and Valentine the maid had both gone down sick: 'Dear Boy, If you will wash dishes, and haunt back kitchens, in the lovely climate of the Eastern States, you must put up with the consequences... 'Tis gay, 'tis romantic, 'tis Bohemian, 'tis even useful and cleanly; but it's too desperate a delight to be often yours.'

Then came a paragraph of jocular congratulations to Louis on being elected a member of the Athenaeum Club, before Henley apologetically turned to his own situation: 'I am out of key today. The spring, sir, is not what it used to be. It amuses, and distresses, me to hear your view of life. "Uncommonly like rot", is it? Have you only just begun to find that out, O Poet of the Counterblast? These three years past I've been entertaining the idea, and it promises to master me. I've work in hand; I owe no more than a

£100; I am beginning to make a reputation; my verse is printing, and promises well enough; other joys [fatherhood] are in store, I believe; and I'd give
the whole lot ten times over for – *enfin!* Life is uncommon like rot. *C'est
convenu.* If it weren't that I am a sort of centre of strength for a number of
feebler folk than myself, I think I'd be shut of it dam soon.'

Knowing the nature of the 'feebler folk' – including Teddy, Henley's
artist brother Anthony and their elderly widowed mother, all of whom
relied on Henley financially – Louis would normally have been sympathetic. Further down the letter, Henley would confess: 'Louis, dear lad,
I am damn tired... The spring is spring no more. I am 39 this year. I am
damn, damn tired. What I want is the wings of a dove – a soiled dove
[prostitute] even! – that I might flee away and be at rest. Don't show this
to *anybody*, and when you write, don't do more than note it in a general
way, if at all. By the time you *do* write you will have forgot all about it, no
doubt. But if you haven't, deal vaguely with my malady. I wish you were
nearer. Why the devil do you go and bury yourself in that bloody country
of dollars and spew?'

But by this point Louis was in no mood to sympathise, having read the
fateful, intervening paragraph. Henley, unable to restrain himself even for
the sake of their friendship, just had to mention the story in *Scribner's*: 'I
read 'The Nixie' with considerable amazement. It's Katharine's; surely it's
Katharine's? The situation, the environment, the principal figure – *voyons!*
There are even reminiscences of phrase and imagery, parallel incident – *que
sais-je?* It is all better-focussed, no doubt; but I think it has lost as much (at
least) as it has gained; and why there wasn't a double signature is what I've
not been able to understand.'

Henley was no doubt bent on mischief, albeit under provocation after all
his efforts to get Katharine's story published. But he never imagined he was
putting a match to a powder magazine that would blow his friendship with
the *Treasure Island* author to smithereens. Louis in a rage could see none
of the dejection and despair of a man who clearly loved him and missed his
company. He saw only an unpardonable attack on his wife, accusing her
of stealing the story from his cousin and depriving Katharine of the much-
needed fee which a double byline would have brought her.

'My dear Henley,' wrote Louis, instead of the 'Dear Lad' that had once
come so naturally. 'I write with indescribable difficulty; and if not with perfect temper, you are to remember how very rarely a husband is expected to
receive such accusations against his wife. I can only direct you to apply to

Katharine and ask her to remind you of that part of the business which took place in your presence and which you seem to have forgotten...'

Claiming that he could not contact Katharine himself because Henley had marked his letter 'Private and Confidential', Louis remounted his high horse and informed his friend:

'I wish I could stop there. I cannot. When you have refreshed your mind as to the facts, you will, I know, withdraw what you have said to me; but I must go further and remind you, if you have spoken of this to others, a proper explanation and retraction of what you have said or implied to any person so addressed, will be necessary.

'From the bottom of my soul, I believe what you wrote to have been merely reckless words written in forgetfulness and with no clear appreciation of their meaning: but it is hard to think that any one – and least of all, my friend – should have been so careless of dealing agony. To have inflicted more distress than you have done would have been difficult. This is the 6th or 7th attempt I make to write to you; and I will now only add that I count upon you immediately applying to Katharine for the facts, and await your answer with the most painful expectation.

'You will pardon me if I can find no form of signature; I pray God such a blank will not be of long endurance, Robert Louis Stevenson.'

William Ernest Henley was not one to suffer a pompous, patronising lecture gladly, and this outburst was hard to take. Such an explosion of Hyde from the genial Jekyll who would normally sign himself 'Yours affectionately, RLS' left him stunned. While knowing he was partly in the wrong, Henley felt no urge to respond quickly with a grovelling apology. Meanwhile Louis was letting off steam in a letter to Charles Baxter about Henley and his 'Shepherd's Bush' gang of hangers-on: 'I fear I have come to an end with Henley; the Lord knows if I have not tried hard to be a friend to him, the Lord knows even that I have not altogether failed. There is not one of that crew that I have not helped in every kind of strait, with money, with service, and that I was not willing to have risked my life for; and yet the years come, and every year there is a fresh outburst against me and mine...'

Convinced that certain friends were turning on him, Louis became obsessed with Henley's 'Private and Confidential' request, raging at the 'baseness of this special form of the anonymous letter'. Nothing would satisfy him but an acknowledgement that Henley had told a lie: 'I have but one clear thought – the desire of wresting an acknowledgement of how the facts stand.' Yet already he confided to Baxter that it would 'probably come to a smash; and I shall have to get you to give the poor creature an allowance'.

Meanwhile Henley, unaware that he was being cast in the role of an ungrateful beggar dependent on Louis's charity, was drafting a letter setting out the facts as he saw them. Knowing how sensitive his friend could be, he had Bob check each sentence for any rash expression that might make matters worse. The 'Private and Confidential' inscription, he explained, 'was meant to cover matters relating only to myself, and had no application to the question at issue, which I had certainly no wish to stifle in our own private circle at least'.

But Henley never sent the letter, because Katharine forbade him to do so. All he could do was complain to Baxter at how exasperated he was by Louis's attitude: 'The immense superiority; the sham set of 'facts'; the assumption that I am necessarily guilty, the complete ignoring of the circumstance that my acquaintance with the case is probably a good deal more intimate and peculiar than his own... all these things have set me wild... I am a person to be ordered about like a common footman, and K. as it were arraigned and put on her defence! It's really incredible.'

Yet the real target for Henley's spleen was Louis's wife, whom he blamed for their estrangement: 'Lewis [sic] has known me longer than his spouse, and has never known me lie or truckle or do anything that is base. He can't have slept with Fanny all these years, and not have caught her in the act of lying.'

Meanwhile, Katharine herself wrote to her cousin, letting her brother check each sentence: 'Dear Louis, As Mr Henley's very natural but unfortunate letter was written without my wish or knowledge, I have refused to let him go further in the matter. He had a perfect right to be astonished but his having said so has nothing to do with me. If Fanny thinks she had a right to the idea of the story I am far from wishing to reclaim or to criticise her in any way. At any rate I cannot be said to have done any wrong or gained anything by the matter, and I therefore refuse to be questioned about it or to let any one else be troubled any further; I am sick to death of the matter and the notion of any quarrel has made me feel quite ill. It is of course very unfortunate that my story was written first and read by people and if they express their astonishment it is a natural consequence and no fault of mine or any one else. I assume that you know me sufficiently to be sure that I have never alluded to the matter even to friends who have spoken of the "Nixie". I trust this matter is not making you feel as ill as all of us. Yours affectionately, Katharine de Mattos.'

Yet there was no affection felt by Louis on reading this, simply anger that Katharine had not confessed it was all her fault. Distraught, he wrote to Baxter: 'A letter has come from Katharine, which shows the case (I fear) to be worse than ever.' Listing the 'facts of the case', he stated that after Katharine's story had been rejected everywhere she then 'wrote and told my wife she might go ahead with her Nixie'. As this letter has not survived, it is impossible to prove which woman was lying. But Louis was now convinced that his cousin, not his friend, was the enemy and in all likelihood Henley had 'only been a handgun for Katharine: who (as you doubtless know) has a great power in that quarter'. Henley's love for Anna was enduring but he did have a soft spot for Katharine, who Louis believed was playing on his friend's chivalrous, protective feelings towards her to keep him 'up to the mark'. In a later letter he would claim Henley had blindly accepted what she had told him, 'passion suppressing many of the facts'. And so, as Louis saw it, 'my poor Knight Errant put lance in rest, and charged – at me'.

Now convinced that Katharine was a Jekyll and Hyde, expressing affection while secretly sowing discord, Louis longed to forgive his friend... if only Henley would confess his error. But although Henley told Baxter he found the situation 'most distressing; and I know not what to say or do', he stood four-square behind Katharine: 'We believe F. stole the story; I believe that K., out of liking for Louis, never made it plain to him that she resented F.'s interference; and having said what I had to say, I should have said no more.' Perhaps overstepping the mark, Henley then lamented that Louis had become involved in a 'hopeless tangle of lies and half-truths which are worse than lies'.

Certainly Louis all but admitted Fanny's guilt when 'in the strictest confidence' he told Baxter: 'This business of the story was (I thought, at the time) silly. Katharine even while she consented – as she did to me with her own lips – expressed unwillingness; I told my wife so; and I asked her to go no further. But she had taken a fancy to the idea, and when Katharine had tried her version and failed and wrote to tell us so, nothing would serve her but to act on this unwilling consent, and try hers. Hers succeeded, and this was trebly vexatious to Katharine, as I clearly see.'

By now Louis was writing to Baxter about changing his will – not to cut Katharine out of it, but to find a way of fulfilling his father's wish that she and Bob should be provided for, without seeming to have forgiven her. He asked Baxter about the possibility of buying an annuity for Katharine's daughter Snoodie – on learning which, Fanny wrote separately to Baxter, urging him to dissuade her husband from such an 'expensive' course of action. Louis himself seemed unaware that handing out money to friends and relations did not always produce the gratitude he expected but could create a sense of shame and resentment at being beholden. In a long letter urging Louis to overlook Henley's 'elephantine tact' and other failings, Baxter observed sagely: 'You have earned great success and fame and money while he remains not only hard up but hampered by the misdeeds of the wretched Teddy. It's not unnatural. Poverty *is* a hard thing, but I think that I have noticed that it is a dangerous thing for a rich man as you now are, or seem to him, to give money, and I'm afraid that the recent gifts which it gave you so much pleasure to suggest, and me to carry out, may have carried a certain gall with them.'

It was a full month after penning the original letter that triggered the quarrel before Henley could find the words to reply to Louis's accusations. His apology was heartfelt: 'My dear Lad, Your letter is heart-breaking; and I do not know how to reply to it, for it convicts me (I now see) of a piece of real unkindness, unworthy of myself and our old tried friendship. You may blame me in the bitterest terms you will for the cruel blunder I made in opening my mind to you; and I shall not complain, for I deserve them all. I should, I know now, have said nothing; and I shall never cease from regretting that I gave you this useless, this unnecessary pain.'

The problem was that Henley would not tell a lie – that he believed Fanny was innocent – and would only offer the assurance: 'It is your mistake, dear lad, to imagine that I've ever been any other than your true friend and servant.' Furious, and still misinterpreting the 'Private and Confidential' inscription, Louis forwarded the letter to Baxter with his own observations on Henley: 'His original position carefully saved throughout; (1) and yet I gave him my word as to certain matters of fact; (2) and yet the letter (in consequence of this) can never be shown to my wife; (3) and yet, even if he still thinks as he did, I think a kind spirit would have lied.'

The last observation was the most telling. It is harder to understand Louis's claim that Fanny could not be shown the correspondence, when less than a fortnight after the original, fateful letter he was telling his wife, away in San Francisco, that 'all my energies have gone in writing and destroying letters to Katharine; but I have now decided after two sleepless nights to do nothing... I wash my hands of these hobgoblin figures, once my friends, for just now.' Fanny was aware of Henley's accusation from the beginning, and was in no doubt why her histrionic husband was crying that he wished he had died at Hyères when they were happy in the South of France.

Not to be outdone, Fanny had hysterics about Katharine's 'treachery' and was convinced she could never show her face in England again after the malicious allegations made against her. 'It's the injustice,' she protested, 'the injustice that eats my soul. How can any one believe that I could rob my dearest friend, the one upon whom I was always seeking to heap benefits.' And when Louis wrote to Katharine, assuring her he would never show her previous letter to Fanny, he received a brief, equally histrionic reply: 'That was best. I am afraid to speak or breathe. There is devilry in the air. K. de M.'

For Louis this was the last straw, and he replied with a full dose of Hyde: 'Dear Katharine, You say "that was best". I thought it best for you. But is that all you have to say? Have you no thanks to make me for an act which I own I thought generous? I suppressed a letter which deeply affected my wife's character from the person most concerned; a letter which if I know anything of life, there is no other human being but myself who would have even tried to pardon; a letter of which (permit me to remind you) you were so much ashamed that you followed it up with two vague notes of apology and deprecation [these have not survived].'

Now in the grip of animal rage, like Hyde bludgeoning Sir Danvers Carew to death, he rained down blow upon blow on his one-time childhood sweetheart: 'I know, and you know, how you have used my wife. I know, and you know, how when this matter came up you failed me with Henley. I know, and you know, how you wrote an answer. I know, and you know, how as soon as you had sent the letter off, your heart misgave you. I know, and you know, how I have sought to spare you till today. I now remind you nakedly of the truth. I do not know how to say what I wish to say. There is always a door open; it is never too late to say I have sinned – if not for others, at least for oneself. God knows my heart is heavy enough with my own offences, to make me sicken at the thought of seeming harsh. But I counsel you, if you wish peace of mind, to do the right thing, and to do it now.'

Then snapping back bizarrely into genial Dr Jekyll mode, he signed himself 'Your old friend and cousin Robert Louis Stevenson'. But if Louis imagined this would bring a tearful, penitent Katharine to him on her knees, he was mistaken. She maintained a wounded silence at her mother's house in Chelsea, leaving Louis to complain to Baxter: 'If there *has* been bad behaviour, hers has certainly been not the least, and I regard her as the wicked mainspring of all this distress.'

After months of this claustrophobic quarrel, Louis could now escape to the wide horizons of the Pacific Ocean and the joys of playing the 'Pirate

Captain (for seven months) of Another Man's Yacht'. Fanny had succeeded in chartering the *Casco* for a voyage from San Francisco through the South Seas to Honolulu. Louis, a little seasick as the yacht swung to anchor off Oakland, dashed off a letter to Baxter. Clearly the quarrel had been patched up with one of the two offending parties, as he wrote: 'I wish you would tell Henley how heartily I have enjoyed his verses. My wife and I were both rejoiced to see him at last do something worthy of himself, as I do think this volume is; some of the pieces are as good as I want to see, both old friends and new.'

Beneath the self-righteous indignation, Louis knew deep down that he had been in the wrong. The row over 'The Nixie' had not been his finest hour, and in a letter to Baxter he had conceded as much: 'I daresay young fellows short of a magazine article in the twentieth century (if our civilisation endures) will expose the horrid RLS and defend and at last do justice to the misused WEH. For he is of that big, round, human, faulty stamp of man that makes lovers after death.'

But his cousin was still unforgiven, with Louis asserting that Fanny, having a special fondness for Katharine, 'was indeed stabbed in the house of her friends'. Louis signed off his letter to Baxter with a self-righteous parting shot: 'To Katharine, if I come again no more, I send these: "It is never too late to repent and make amends."'

At 5am on 28 June 1888, the *Casco* headed out through the Golden Gate bound for the Marquesas, the Paumotus and Tahiti. At sea Louis experienced good health for the first time in many years. But the cancer of his soured relationship with the cousin who had once been so close to him would never be cured. Katharine herself acknowledged this in one final letter that caught up with the *Casco* when it reached Honolulu the following January. Despairingly she wrote: 'I know this can *never* get better, but perhaps nothing can make it worse. So do listen when I once more assure you of my entire ignorance that Mr Henley was writing. If I had wished to write or speak to anyone on the subject I could have done it myself but I never had any wish to do so... I don't think I exaggerate when I say I was maddened with despair when I read your letter which taxed me with a dreadful preconceived plot. I can only myself know how impossible it would have been to me to do such a thing. How deeply sorry I am it is useless to try to say and impossible not to remember all your past kindness which has now turned into a life long distrust of me. If I have failed to understand anything said to me at Bournemouth or put a wrong construction on things I am more grieved than ever but I cannot say it has been intentional. Katharine de Mattos.'

This was still not the repentance and amends that Louis had demanded, and any love he once had for his cousin would now be a thing of the past. In one last terse comment from Honolulu he told Baxter: 'As for Katharine, I had an answer to my appeal, which settled that matter: I do not wish to see her.'

# 11

# In Her Own Write

IN CHELSEA LIFE went on as before for Katharine as she continued her literary journalism while bringing up Snoodie and Richard. But there was one significant change. The break-up with Louis had cost her the friendship of Henley, too. Fourteen years after the quarrel, Katharine would reveal the full tragedy arising from the one-legged man's rash comments: 'That letter was written without my knowledge and unfortunately after I had already written to Fanny saying I had seen *Scribner* and thought the story well managed. I also spoke of it to friends of hers and mine in the same way. I said to my mother that, whatever we felt about it, this should be our tone on Louis's account. I did in fact – though in vain – just what he would have desired and expected from a friend and cousin.

'I had no idea that Mr Henley had grudges of his own or that his action was not prompted by wrong headed kindness to me and because he had charge of the story in question. He had helped me more than once to place articles and to find work. We had a dreadful scene in which I said I considered his conduct dishonourable and he said I should be "betraying" him – "Henley" – if I vindicated Louis and family in the matter. We seldom met after that time and never cordially. I have not seen him for years.'

Shortly after this showdown, Henley's life took on a new dimension with the birth of his daughter Margaret and a new editor's berth for himself – in Edinburgh, where a paper called the *Scots Observer* was being launched. He and his family moved into a house in Howard Place, the street where Louis was born. By now Louis had forgiven his old friend and from Honolulu sent his congratulations on the birth of the baby: 'I trust she will grow up strong and good and happy, and be all you now dream of.' Even Fanny seemed pleased, at least for the sake of her husband, and was delighted to receive a photograph of little Margaret. Louis wrote back: 'I handed the daughter without one word to my wife. "Henley without his clothes!" cried she. The resemblance is killing.'

Yet none of this reached the ears of Katharine, who sought refuge in work. She now had regular commissions from *The Athenaeum*, which was a big payer, and could earn £10 for a weekly book review. It may have given her some satisfaction to know her income was now five times that of the husband who had ill-treated her for so long. Since the founding of the Fabian Society, Sydney de Mattos had been joint secretary along with a house-painter called Philips. Later he became the society's lecture secretary, organising talks around the country, for which he received £2 a week plus expenses. When not touring the provinces in the name of socialism and in search of free love, de Mattos occupied furnished bachelor quarters in Lavender Sweep, Battersea, for which he paid 9/6d a week.

Bob, despite his involvement in Katharine and Henley's fateful letters to Louis, continued to correspond with his cousin, albeit awkwardly. This may have been influenced by Louisa's dislike of her husband's cousin. Although nearly all men and most women fell under the spell of Louis's charismatic personality, a few remained immune to his charm. Perhaps having glimpsed his Hyde side in the letters to her sister-in-law, Louisa may have been less inclined than Bob to overlook it – particularly when Katharine was a welcome visitor at their West Kensington home where the presence of a baby nephew had helped keep the upset over 'The Nixie' in perspective.

Born a few days before Henley's fateful letter, Alan Louis Stevenson was the son on whom Bob pinned all his hopes. Yet by September 1888, when Louis was on the high seas, Bob was writing to him with tragic news of the child named after him: 'I am sorry to say that Alan has died at the age of nearly seven months. It is a good thing for him as upon a post-mortem being made it was found that he had only one kidney and consequently could not have lived, or for a short time miserably. He was otherwise very strong and sound in heart and lungs etc. It is of course a sad affair for us. I had hoped that he might have turned out well. There is good stuff in the family and though I have not shown much of it I suppose I might have transmitted latent capability. However, that must pass; we cannot expect to have everything our own way and things might have turned out badly. As to the boy, of course, it was well for him to die before he began to suffer as he would have done.'

As an artist Bob had to accept failure, but with Henley's help he had carved a niche for himself as an art critic for the Saturday Review, where he wrote music reviews also. Now in the letter announcing the death of little Alan Louis, he wrote without enthusiasm about his new job as Roscoe

Professor of Fine Art at Liverpool university: 'I have to begin the lectures in October at Liverpool and feel rather alarmed I have nothing ready but must trust a good deal to inspiration and luck. There is much to do... and these Liverpool people have made me one of the secretaries of a big Congress on Art on the lines of the British Association: You may figure my uselessness and my disgust, and I may add my disbelief.'

Bob stuck it for three years before handing in his resignation, telling a friend: 'I was expected to wear a high hat and a carnation in my buttonhole, and talk mild gossip about Botticelli, Burne-Jones and Frith – actually Frith – at garden parties and afternoon teas... I held out as long as I could and then I simply cut it, for no human being could have stood it any longer.'

Into those three years, on the other side of the globe, Louis crammed a lifetime of living that had been denied him for so long in the sickroom. Suntanned, fit and free from haemorrhages in the tropics, he embarked on further Boy's Own adventures in the South Seas, encountering storms at sea and former cannibals before settling at last in Samoa. There, in his big new plantation house called Vailima, he began at the start of 1892 to write the sequel to *Kidnapped*. Its heroine was to be Katriona, altered in the final version to Catriona, the Gaelic version of Katharine. Was Louis thinking of his estranged cousin when he created her, or was it mere coincidence?

As Catriona took shape in Samoa, a slim volume by Katharine was published at last by T. Fisher Unwin in London and Cassell in New York. Each publisher produced a series of books – the *Pseudonym Library* and the *'Unknown' Library* – by authors not wishing to use their own names. Appearing in both under the male pseudonym 'Theodor Hertz-Garten', Katharine could never be accused of trading on her famous cousin's name as Fanny Stevenson had done. Louis might have recognised the title – *Through The Red-Litten Windows* – but there is no evidence that he ever saw a copy or even realised Katharine was a published author at last.

Her book contains just two stories, the earlier horror tale rooted in *Jekyll and Hyde* and a novella called *The Old River House*. The house is in Chelsea by the Thames, dispensing with the grounds of the Royal Hospital with its red-coated pensioners which separated Aunt Alan's home in St Leonard's Terrace from the river. In the story it is the home of the widowed Susan Grey, her son Leonard and daughter Avis, both of whom are artistic and play the piano that once belonged to their late father. They keep open house to a variety of young friends who like to think they stay abreast of every development in art, music and literature, while finding it impossible to elicit an opinion of any sort from the impassive Mrs Grey.

Into this glittering company steps Leonard and Avis's cousin. In Katharine's imagination he had once been Dick Turpin, the Knight of the Road whose manly arms rescued her from teenage despair after losing her father. Then he became Dick Naseby, who fell for Esther van Tromp or Fanny Vandegrift Osbourne in *The Story of a Lie*. Later he would turn himself into Dick Shelton, the hero of *The Black Arrow*, sharing adventures with a tomboy not unlike Katharine's adolescent self. Now it was her turn to fictionalise Louis – as the successful artist Dick Shadwell, a family friend and cousin of Leonard and Avis.

However much Katharine may have been hurt by the letters from America, there is no rancour towards Louis in her fictional portrayal, only love, adoration… and pity for the man who once addressed the original version of the *Jekyll and Hyde* dedication to her with words of affection and the salutation 'Ave!' If it must be 'hail and farewell' to their relationship, at least she felt no bitterness towards him. As Avis sits playing the piano, pouring her soul into the music, Shadwell feels strongly drawn towards her but knows nothing can come of it – because he is married already.

Fictionalising Fanny was another matter. In revenge for the Nixie stolen from an asylum, Katharine would put Shadwell's wife there instead. Dick is to be pitied because he is shackled to a madwoman. Through the power of fiction, Katharine has Fanny the Bedlamite locked away like Mrs Rochester. What she would never know was how near this piece of wish-fulfilment came to the truth. Ten thousand miles away, Louis, Belle and Lloyd were beginning to have serious fears for Fanny's sanity.

She had always been prone to strong emotions, fierce loyalties and implacable hatreds, as Louis jokingly warned JM Barrie, then contemplating a trip to Samoa: 'If you don't get on with her, it's a pity about your visit. She runs the show. Infinitely little, extraordinary wig of gray curls, handsome waxen face like Napoleon's, insane black eyes, boy's hands, tiny bare feet, a cigarette, wild blue native dress usually spotted with garden mould. In company manners presents the appearance of a little timid and precise old maid of the days of prunes and prism; you look for the reticule… A violent friend, a brimstone enemy. Imaginary conversation after your visit: "I like Mr Barrie. I don't like anybody else. I don't like anybody that don't like him…" Is always either loathed or slavishly adored; indifference impossible. The natives think her uncanny and that devils serve her. Dreams dreams, and sees visions.'

But behind the joking lay real worry, for shortly before publication of Katharine's book, Fanny had begun to show signs of mental illness. Louis confided only in his old friend Sidney Colvin: 'Fanny is not well, and we are miserably anxious. I may as well say now that for nearly 18 months there has been something wrong; I could not write of it; but it was very trying and painful – and mostly fell on me... The doctor has given her a medicine; we think it too strong, yet dare not stop it; and she passes from deathbed scenes to states of stupor. Ross, doctor in Sydney, warned me to expect trouble, so I'm not surprised; and happily Lloyd and Belle and I work together very smoothly, and none of us get excited... You know about F. there's nothing you can say is wrong, only it ain't right; it ain't she; at first she annoyed me dreadfully; now of course, that one understands, it is more anxious and pitiful.

'Later. 1.30. The doctor has been. "There is no danger to life," he said twice. – "Is there any danger to mind?" I asked. – "That is not excluded," said he. Since then I have had a scene with which I need not harrow you; and now again she is quiet and seems without illusions. 'Tis a beastly business... At first it only seemed a kind of set against me; she made every talk an argument, then a quarrel; till I fled her, and lived in a kind of isolation in my own room... The last was a hell of a scene which lasted all night – I will never tell anyone what about, it could not be believed, and was so unlike herself or any of us – in which Belle and I held her for about two hours; she wanted to run away. Then we took her to Sydney; and the first few weeks were delightful: her voice quiet again – no more of that anxious shrillness about nothing that had so long echoed in my ears. And then she got bad again. Since she has been back, also she has been kind – querulously so, but kind. And today's fit (which was the most insane she has yet had) was still only gentle and melancholy.

'Friday April 7: I am thankful to say the new medicine quieted her at once; and she has been entirely reasonable and very nice since she took it... We have got her back to her own room where Belle sleeps with her. Belle and I are to take watches all day, off and on, to be with her.'

Had Katharine known all this, she would never have wished it on her cousin, even fictionally. All she knew was that Louis was shackled to Fanny for good – and however much Katharine's alter ego Avis may yearn for Shadwell in the story, she knows the situation can never get better and must end in tragedy.

The fictional tragedy hinges on her brother – Bob the artist transformed into Leonard the composer. Leonard falls desperately in love with the beautiful Gwendolen Brook, who, like Belle, is incapable of loving him in return. Suddenly his art is meaningless and he shuts himself away in his room in bleak despair. But there is no Louisa Purland to rescue him from the downward spiral into drug addiction and, ultimately, suicide. The tragedy ends in the cemetery, which Shadwell visits regularly with his aunt, the one member of the family with whom he still has contact. And Dick's wife, Katharine notes with grim satisfaction, remains incarcerated, sometimes unable even to recognise her unfortunate husband: 'Sometimes she only shuddered at the sight of him with a nameless, meaningless fear; at others she raved wildly, her wrecked beauty aflame with the fire of unquenchable madness.'

# 12

# Tragedy Transformed

IT IS STRANGE to think of Katharine at her mother's house in Chelsea, struggling to make sense of her life – the wrecked marriage, the joys and worries of single parenthood, the struggle to earn a living as one of the first lady journalists, mixing with some of the most talented creative artists in the country... and behind it all the dull ache of knowing that Louis would never forgive her. All she could do was transform the tragedy of love, friendship and estrangement into a work of art. Katharine's tale is no masterpiece, but she did take her own girlish longings, the dashed dreams of her brother and the lost love of her cousin married to a temperamental rival, and endow them with a haunting beauty:

## *The Old River House*
By Katharine de Mattos

## *By The River*

THE afternoon sunshine streamed through amber-coloured draperies and flooded the drawing-room of an old house a little apart from others by the great river. A giant wisteria – one of those supposed to have been planted years ago by the hands of French emigrants, and nowhere in greater perfection than in Chelsea – disputed with an ancient vine the frontage of the house. Bound together in a close and vital embrace, the two went racing and rioting to the topmost chimney. Amidst the gnarled and twisted branches birds built their nests, and with twitterings and chirpings broke a silence which, but for the far-off tumult of the streets, would have rivalled the silence of the country itself.

Today the great room, running from front to back of the house, was animated by unwonted influences. Ribbons and laces fluttered, gay gowns moved hither and hither, accentuating the soberer raiment of men. A hum of voices, a sheen of moving brightness, and the triumphant hue of pyramids of glowing flowers woke into sudden life, almost into gaiety, the shadowy nooks of the dark-panelled, low-ceilinged rooms.

Everywhere there were people – mostly young people – changing places, grouping and regrouping like a series of dissolving views. Chatting and laughing, they moved about handing tea or strawberries; others, not so active, leaned on the vine-covered balconies absorbed in conversation; while those not talkatively disposed amused themselves by looking out on the wide waterway, vaguely or appreciatively aware of the movement and life thereon. The brown-sailed, green-bodied crafts plied their way downstream, an idle coal barge loomed stately in the softening haze ere it slipped slowly beneath the bridge. Everything seemed to have a character, an impressiveness of its own, due, in reality, to the swiftly changing effects of sky and water, and the constant play of light and shadow.

A good many people were beginning to discover pleasant possibilities in and about the Old River House. It was, as it were, out of their usual beat, it was unlike other places, and yet they liked it. Visitors did much as they pleased. There was no herding of 'the right people' together, no penning up of others – little or no management, in fact. Yet the results were good, sometimes even brilliant. As a hostess Mrs Grey did not shine; far from it. She was one of those provoking people on whom a handsome face and good natural 'carriage' are entirely thrown away. She was elderly, certainly; but women twice as elderly, with the least hit of science, would have got a vast deal more out of her advantages than she did. She looked as though she had never in her life put a discriminating touch to her cap, hair, or any other adjunct of her person. She 'just put her things on' – so do other people, but they make some attempt 'wearing' them. Mrs Grey made none. She was a singularly impassive, silent being, who might have detracted seriously from the animation of any gathering in which she was concerned, had it not been that, after five minutes or so, people forgot her impressive aspect, and learned to look on her as a finished piece of architecture rather than as a human being and a hostess.

If she was aware of her own shortcomings they did not trouble her the least. She felt no interest in, or responsibility for, the guests – they were her son Leonard's, not hers. For herself she had no desire either for society, or for friends. She put up with them, but she did not seek them. These were, besides, the kind of guests who may be trusted to amuse themselves; they would have amused her, too, had such a thing not been a manifest impossibility. She had never been amused in her life, nor felt the need of amusement, and she had no idea of making experiments with herself now. Her daughter's airs were gentler, though less inert, but she gave promise of developing more aptitude than her mother in the art of entertaining. She had not long reached the 'grown-up' stage of existence, however, and little was expected of her.

Her son Leonard made up for their deficiencies. He seemed to be more natural, more like other people. Without being fussy or formal he was everywhere at once, looking after things, and enjoying himself in a special manner besides. In outward appearance he was not unlike his mother, but his face was full of the fire and expression hers lacked, so that the resemblance was altogether physical and superficial. His eyes testified, just then, to an enjoyment, almost to a delight, hardly warranted by the scene around him; yet it was in part explained when they turned often, as though instinctively, in the direction of a young and very beautiful girl who strove to entertain rather than to be entertained by his mother. The Greys had all fine, but not very discerning eyes, and Leonard would probably have remained delightfully ignorant that anything was amiss, even if Miss Brook had not been what she was – a past mistress in the art of making conversation. To him it only seemed that the two were getting on together 'wonderfully well'.

Certain people, without appearing to watch, hovered in the neighbourhood, talking amongst themselves, yet noting every turn of the situation. They had acquired the habit of seeming absorbed in one thing, while in reality alive to another. It was generally something of a temptation to visitors to note how newcomers came through their ordeal with Mrs Grey – in this case the temptation was irresistible.

Gwendolen Brook was an acknowledged beauty – in itself enough to keep a small and subdued stir constantly about her. At present she appeared heart and soul absorbed in Mrs Grey's rare, monosyllabic, and most uninspiring answers to her own deft and tactful remarks. It was a radiant face, radiant in expression as well as in colouring, that she turned on her companion's massive, well-appointed countenance, and none save a keen observer would have guessed that she was finding her first meeting with her hostess somewhat uphill work. Hitherto she had managed life and every one in it like a charm, and such an experience as a repulse was new to her. Amongst her many and varied accomplishments she had made a specialty of one. She was unusually good at drawing out and setting at their ease unfortunate people of both sexes, who had not her delightful talents. Socially speaking, Mrs Grey's was not an easy 'case'. She had none of the shyness, flurry, nor absent-mindedness which sometimes mark even the elderly recluse. A settled and somewhat ominous calm, an absolute detachment, and an over-whelming passivity, capable of turning aside the most insinuating weapons of attack, were her distinguishing traits. To know where to have a person to whom the ordinary amenities of conversation seem a dead, or at least a lost, language is not easy. 'Farouche', as the girl would herself have expressed it, she was not. She was too sincerely uninterested in the world's verdicts to be that. Neither was she actively contradictory, nor could she, truthfully speaking, be called acquiescent.

She was only 'not very sure' of anything Miss Brook advanced. To begin with, she was not 'at all sure' that hers was such, a 'very charming old house', nor, though she did not say it in so many words, that she found it improved since the caprices of fashionable folk had broken in on its shadowy silence, metamorphosing it into the life and tumult of today. Some newcomers had, on a first visit, informed her, with a sweet, sophisticated candour all their own, how they 'adored' her son's music – himself, even – and how 'more than charmed' they were to meet his mother. Their remarks had fallen to the ground. Now this girl seemed to be telling her the same thing, or something like it, only less crudely – and succeeding no better than the rest.

Yet somehow, in spite of reverses, people came and came again, reporting the place to their acquaintance as 'delightfully quaint and unconventional, don't you know!' so 'ideal and artistic', so in keeping with Leonard Grey, who, with his touch of the 'romantic air', was all a young musician and com-poser should be – from their point of view. Their view was not Mrs Grey's. When she studied her son it was with perplexity rather than pleasure. As a rule, however, she did not study him; she let him alone. Yet in a speechless, subterranean, and wholly inexplicable way of her own, she was fond of him.

In time quite a stream of people found their way to the Greys. Clever women and 'society women' appeared there, women less talented and less socially distinguished also flocked thither, armed with little rolls of MS or violin cases – those cases we see blocking the railway stations, and swelling the traffic of our streets. Young men, reported to have made their conver-sation 'an art', and who valued themselves accordingly, dashed up in han-soms on many an afternoon or evening. Whether they wore their hair almost shockingly short, or a little too long, or cultivated no hair at all, they seemed inclined to strike an 'individual note of their own' in that as in more essen-tial matters. Gifted authors of the male and female persuasion 'looked in'; critics, musical, dramatic, and literary, with other representatives of the New Journalism, went in and out, finding pasture according to his or her kind.

Above the clangour of the street, and the sounds from the dreaming river, there rose now from the once quiet house a babel of tongues, a burst of song and laughter, all the signs and tokens that show 'society' is amusing itself.

Leaning back in her low chair, a quite entrancing hat casting a shadowy softness on her charming features, her figure slightly obscured by her companion's large, unimpressionable presence, Gwendolen Brook continued to find it uphill work. In despair she had long ago abandoned the notion of taking Mrs Grey captive by any of her usual methods. She could only trust to her frank, spontaneous ease of manner to keep the secret of her discomfiture from others. She liked what she had seen of Leonard; she was attracted by something in him novel and unlike the people she was accustomed to meet, and she had allowed herself the seemingly innocent caprice of learning something more of his family and surroundings. Her idea had been to come, to see, and to conquer the whole environment, but time passed and no sign of capitulation was given. Sundry proofs and evidences of Leonard's talent; his talk about his mother – in sober truth there had not been any – and her consequent desire to know her, were sweetly reviewed, only to fall like spent arrows against the solid buttress of Mrs Grey's impenetrability.

'It must be good for him,' the girl went on; still using her persuasive voice, 'to be taken away from his work now and then, from his splendid thoughts, and – and all that, even by frivolous people. Don't you agree with me, dear Mrs Grey?' She paused and sighed, perhaps for a missing word, perhaps for some sign or symptom of encouragement. 'To be obliged to turn from his dreams and aspirations, to have to encounter the average man and woman, and to hustle them from the dead level of their Philistinism, *must* be good. It is good for them, at any rate, you must allow.'

She paused. She really feared she was beginning to talk incoherent nonsense, yet she went on with an air of animated conviction and brightness which should have won an uncritical hearer – especially a mother. But Mrs Grey, always unwilling to commit herself to an expression of opinion, however trifling, was now more wooden than usual.

Her own children were accustomed to her; they seldom or never asked her a question, scarcely even as to what she would eat or drink, or wherewithal she would be clothed. It was useless. Either she did 'not quite know', or she 'would see', or 'really she thought it was not worthwhile to get anything just then'. Even on such a question as the opening or shutting of a door she contrived to cast a doubt on the truth of the saying that a door must be shut or open. It was impossible her children should realise that her mute life had a meaning and significance of its own; that obscure and reiterated sorrows had helped to make her what she was, and had robbed her of a vitality never too strong. It was doubt and uncertainty rather than indifference and coldness that had at first sealed her lips and taught her to walk softly all her days, crystallised into abnormal apathy and inertia. She vaguely felt – definite feelings were impossible to her – that Gwendolen Brook, and the society to which she belonged, could do Leonard even less good than the world of art which she also distrusted; in that world her dead husband had long ago been alienated from her, making shipwreck of what faith and hope she possessed. In her crushed and helpless way she was perhaps thinking of all this, but the girl at her side could know nothing of it. She was only a little surprised and piqued, perhaps a shade impatient with the strange person who was responsible for her unwonted feelings. She hated the prying eyes which 'take in' situations, and which were still watching the development of what would have long ago proved with most people a hopeless conversational impasse. They must not, if she could help it, discover her defeat. It was therefore in such a manner as to make her escape look not unlike a triumph that she presently vanished to another part of the room, carrying with her a satellite or two who had been watching their opportunity.

It is sometimes as difficult to be delivered from the hands of friends as of enemies. Dick Shadwell, friend and cousin of the house, had found it so amongst these new acquaintances of the Greys, some of whom proved to be old ones of his own. He had detached himself from group after group, slipping easily and gracefully from each detaining hand, till at length he found himself alone.

More than one thing had of late drawn the Greys and himself together. He counted it no hardship to be often with them. He was changed since the days when he thought it 'a bore', and Mrs Grey the dullest of all dull aunts – and women, too. He had pitied *feu* Mr Grey, and sympathised with him for finding no better refuge than music from the monotony of his fate. He was thinking how his own misfortunes had changed him since then, when he overheard words not meant to reach his ears.

'It's rough on him, poor old chap,' a voice was saying, in friendly tones that were familiar to him. 'He hardly shows anywhere nowadays; makes "no moan", but takes it hard. His wife – beautiful woman she was – something wrong with the brain, you know.' The listener felt rather than saw the gesture. 'Shadwell doesn't seek the con-solations the gods – or others – provide.

Not that sort, though we shouldn't have guessed it once on a time, should we, eh? Poor old Dick!'

Here Shadwell, who had got uncomfortably sandwiched between a three-cornered table and an angular lady, managed to move on unobserved. He had heard enough.

Life had assumed a sterner complexion; he had known worse evils than dullness since the days when he had shrunk from what he used to call the 'muffled atmosphere' of the Old River House. It soothed and interested him nowadays to watch the current of these lives, to note how the impetuous stream of the younger man's existence chafed against its narrow limits as his own had once done. He saw him introduce new elements into the hushed and quiet household, and wondered how it would answer. Insensibly he had grown into a very faithful friend of the family, and few days passed that did not see them together. Leonard often declared that he could not get on without him. His greater experience of the world, and of life generally, were precious to the young man at this stage of his existence. In her negative way his aunt was not unkind to him, and he liked her now, and understood her better than others did; servants, for instance, who left her for no other reason than that they could not 'abear' the deep repose of the head of the family.

Today Shadwell felt that the claims of relationship and friendship were satisfied, that his social duties were done. Materially and intellectually he had, to the best of his ability, fed the hungry, and not himself gone empty away. He was observant of the aspect and humours of his fellow-creatures, whoever and wherever they might be. Richard Shadwell's was a pleasant, kindly face, yet with something trenchant about it, too; the face of a man who knows how to smile at his own as well as other people's follies. He had handed ices and cakes, talked Impressionist and Rival schools with an eclectic and intelligent painter, had listened to views on Ibsen and the advanced playwriters, and the possibility of a Free and Independent theatre; the tendencies of latter-day life and fiction had been discussed with a group of youthful 'literati' of light and leading, and, above all, he had suffered himself to be interviewed (in earnest, by a lady) on the faith that was in him with regard to the 'higher planes of existence', and the rightful interpretation of true altruism. He had a dim recollection of having met this lady in what now really seemed a former state of existence; when he had been gayer-hearted, and she had been a – Positivist! Religions and individuals develop quickly nowadays. Here, too, he had come across Gwendolen Brook – '*que diable fait elle dans cette galére?*' he softly and unchivalrously murmured, watching from afar her gay and once familiar spiritings.

He stopped now and again in his thoughtful progress through the rooms to look at people or to handle some bit of modern decoration, a vase, or hanging which Leonard, bent on the 'adornment of the home', had imported and fused, not always skilfully, with surroundings bearing evidence of an earlier and severer taste. He knew his kinswomen to be unfemininely devoid of feeling for beauty of this sort, almost ludicrously out of date, in such matters. He smiled a little as he turned about things new and old, ivory figures under glass, flanked by Leonard's copious and daring arrangements in flowers, presentation copies of brand-new verses or essays, and a fantastically realistic sketch or two, signatures in themselves of painters supposed to speak the latest word on art. Leonard had, it would seem, struck into the 'movement' with more zeal than discretion, carrying his household with him as far as possible.

Shadwell at length came to anchor in the deep embrasure of a deserted window at the back of the house. It gave on to the usual London 'garden', grown in this case, through neglect or design, into something resembling a miniature wilderness. Flooded in afternoon sunshine it looked pretty enough; tall weeds, and flowers on the borderland between cultivation and nature, twining or straggling about the blackened stems of blossoming limes.

The sound of a low chord, followed by a momentary pause in the many-headed buzz of conversation in the far end of the room, broke in on his reflections and made him turn to see who was usurping the pianoforte. It stood on the far side of the window in a wide recess, surrounded by big palms and other plants; the sun shedding solemn light on its tall, polished body. Before it, seated on the narrow, carved bench, he saw his young cousin, Avis Grey. The talk, scarce broken off, went on again immediately, as though the talkers instinctively guessed from the character of the music that their attention was not needed or claimed. Few present knew the girl. Hers was not the sort of adolescence likely to draw their observation. She was subdued and silent, without any 'ways' of her own, or 'pretty manners' that might recommend her. Her unheeded and isolated chords had gradually passed into a. hushed accompaniment to a low, half-brooding song. Screened by the surrounding greenery, she sang on, evidently to herself alone, without thought of the other room and its occupants. What she sang was new to Shadwell. Above the noise of talk and talkers he only made out words here and there –

'*Il m'est doux de dormir, et plus doux d'être de marbre... je ne veux pas voir ni entendre; ainsi donc ne m'éveille pas; de gràce parle bas.*' This or something like it he caught now and again, and the air, a kind of *recitative*, the words, the tone of the voice, all sounded new and unfamiliar in his ears. He lingered; the music, the girl's quiet presence, were pleasant to him then.

The pianoforte was German, old-fashioned, even antique in make. In spite of age and use it seemed to deepen rather than lose in strength and tone. He looked on it with a sort of curiosity as having belonged to 'poor old Grey', as he somewhat disrespectfully termed his relative when he chanced to think of him. He was not himself fond of the pianoforte as an instrument, and he had sometimes laughed at his cousins' devotion to this one – a devotion their mother did not share.

Many were the arguments he and Leonard had on the subject of music, and pianofortes in particular. He thought them limited and defective. The younger man admitted the limitations as, to a certain extent, inseparable from the nature of the instrument, yet declared that the want of power and insight in performers should be taken into account. He had a theory (very seriously maintained) that sundry new and undiscovered combinations of sound, added to an finer and more discriminating touch, must in time bring into play factors now dormant and only waiting the call to action. He declared that in their own pianoforte he heard mysterious tones promising a solution and fulfilment of some kind. Shadwell admitted that pianos are aggravatingly full of suggestion and promise of a something that never comes, that never will come; this, he alleged, is the nature of the instrument – and its charm! Leonard's eloquence was often brought to bear on him, but he still cited famous pianists, and maintained that no more could be got out of the scheme and scope of a single instrument constructed on such a plan. It was scientifically, it was humanly impossible...

On the top of the pianoforte stood a quaint old mirror, beneath were rare china bowls dispensing the fragrance of dead roses. The wood was so dark and highly polished that Shadwell could see reflected in it, nearly to the waist, the young musician's white-robed figure. Sprays of flame-coloured flowers, on a projecting bracket, cast a deep glow on the reflection of her white gown. It was a finished picture the clear depths returned to him; a picture full of grace and far-off mystery. The strength and power of the reflection impressed him for the first time. It stimulated his fancy as a new light cast on seemingly familiar objects always does. In those clear yet apparently far-away depths, in that unsubstantial but perfectly defined image, he felt a hint of something new and strange that affected the personality of his little cousin. He had looked on her as a mere accessory of her brother, as a being devoted to and inseparable from his larger, stronger vitality. Her own life seemed to have been always contentedly or unconsciously merged in his. Now, into the unknown melody there crept, or so he thought, an undercurrent of her own feeling, sweet and strange, broken-winged yet seeking to soar. The fair hair rolled halo-wise from her quiet brow, the lowered eyelids touched with a thought of impalpable grace and beauty; all seemed new to him. She continued to play, and playing appeared, as it were, to have fallen more and more away from her old self, to be gazing, not into, but through her own reflection at something beyond, above it. He fell to wondering what those lowered eyes concealed, what that something was so fain to pierce through them. The singing mouth, the parted, longing lips pouring forth that flood of hushed melody, surely in them was an accent that strove to discover, to point a way somewhere – somewhere where none might follow. Towards the same goal the pianoforte seemed gradually to yearn and strain with subdued yet hidden energy. No one heeded the sounds, no one moved to the magic of the voice save himself, a man seemingly sober and sparing of his emotions. Was the atmosphere of the River House making him dreamy and fanciful? Was he growing imaginative? What harm if he were, so no one suffered from his fancies?

As on a painting at which you steadfastly gaze till it appears about to change beneath your eyes, as if eager to reveal the secret spring of its being, though it must still leave the beholder aloof and apart, so Shadwell gazed on and on. What he saw was but the reflection, in a leaf of wood, of a familiar face, but it seemed more vivid, more real than reality, yet altogether new and unfamiliar. It seemed the presentation and image of a life very far off, not bearing on his own; an existence on which time, as we know it, may not act or press. Could there be anything, after, all, in his cousin's wild notions as to the secret power of instrument and player when rightly matched? Could it be this girl, whom he saw almost daily on her quiet round of household tasks, this little Avis – white of heart and soul – who was destined to become the revealer of anything occult or withheld?

The sunset climax was approaching. Its dying fire touched the reflection with a transient gleam, turning the crimson flowers into a trail of glory over the white bosom of her gown. His excited fancy saw, not Avis, but a fair-winged, unearthly player, a young virgin making melody before the lord of an unknown kingdom. Then his mental gaze passed beyond her – out, whither he knew not, seeking the wild, unsaintly beauty of another face – a face he dared not now think upon… The girl's music had begun to assume a more halting and chaotic character. His wandering attention went back to her. She sat straight up, and her eyes plunged into the old mirror above her head, which reflected the further room. What did she see there that made her lips tremulous, and her fingers rest idly on the keys? He only saw a knot of people: Leonard, Miss Brook, with the friends who had brought her, and were just taking their leave.

'Since you really like the place so much, you will surely come again soon,' the young man was saying, quite simply and earnestly. 'You can see the old church, and the hospital, or we might – '

'Explore "the other objects of interest in the neighbourhood" – the very thing,' the girl broke in rapidly and lightly. 'You must tell me all the histories. I promise to be interested beforehand.'

There was little to see, little to hear in all this; it was an ordinary enough parting. But Avis, who had now quite ceased playing, seemed to have seen more in the mirrored movements of the little group: her brother's repressed yet adoring gaze, and the back-turned movement of the girl's lovely head. They passed from her line of vision, yet her gaze lingered on the mirror as though sad earth visions instead of dreams of a slumbrous paradise haunted her now. Would she, he mused, be always content to remain thus, a spectator at life's banquet, a Lady of Shallott, whose safety, perhaps, lay in a life of shadows? He sighed a little for her, perhaps, perhaps for his own life. Then he roused himself. He felt he was on the brink of some feeling it was not well to encourage. What was that plaintive song of hers about *'ne m'éveille donc pas; de grâce parle bas'*? Poor child! He would not be the one to awake her, he who had no right to part or lot in any save one woman's life. And that one hopelessly mad!

The dying flush had faded from the sky, the glamour had passed from the picture, leaving the girl and her reflection wan and white. He spoke her name softly over her shoulder, and with a slight start and a soft cry of 'Oh, Dick, is it you?' she turned to him as though reluctantly. The spell broke, it was only little Avis Grey, all unidealised, who showed her face. What should he feel for her but the mildest, kindliest affection? What was there in her face, now, that he did not know by heart – or think he did? How well, indeed, he seemed to know her attitude, sitting there, a small, stiff figure, with none of the rounded grace of early girlhood; instead, in some of her lines, a whimsical suggestion, a sort of affinity with the old pianoforte itself, with its slender, high-backed, rather angular outlines.

## On The River

TWILIGHT was deepening into night. In spite of the rapidly freshening air, Leonard Grey did not appear inclined to retreat from the open window. A succession of men friends had been about the River House the greater part of the afternoon. They had little to do themselves, and did not realise that other people were not in a like case. But he was alone at length. The last determined straggler, always too much with us at the close of day, had retired. Yet he did not move. Seen by yellow lamplight the blue haze without showed like a vast parterre, scattered lights beginning to twinkle and blossom far off across the waste of waters. Land and river lay undistinguishably blended, or defined only by the coloured lights of the bridges, looking like great jewelled necklaces flung airily across space.

No one came to disturb the young man; he was alone with his dreams. Some time back Avis had been kindly, but somewhat cavalierly, dismissed on the plea of work, which he now seemed in no hurry to be at. He had seen Gwendolen Brook some hours back, and his face was still alight with the joy of remembrance and expectation. At length he rose, but it was only to turn down the lamps and seat himself at the old pianoforte. For a moment he touched the keys as though in doubt, then something triumphal floated out to the quiet stars. Tonight the instrument seemed to respond to his touch as never before in all his strivings to reach the innermost quick of its being. Surely something of his best manner, with a superadded power, had come to him once more. He thought so, as he went on pouring out his happiness with lavish touch, the notes vibrating as with a promise of fulfilment. Tonight all things seemed possible; his love would be requited, his musical quest rewarded!

Gradually his first exaltation fell, and a less personal strain crept into the music. The blight and swarm of trivial interests and endeavours his love had forced him to stem, that had, unknown to himself, been marring his compositions, took flight. 'A nobler, calmer train of feeling' succeeded. As though summoned by enchantment, an invisible choir of immortals seemed to hover near him, and for once he felt not unworthy of their presence. A tone of mild and beautiful persistence ran more and more through the music, a current of untainted love and enjoyment of youth and nature purged it of fiercer and more personal aspirations. He thought he detected in the instrument a still more persuasive yet elusive utterance, as though it were on the point of revealing yet postponing its secret...

'This, this is *heaven*!' stammered the young man in ecstasy, his face, that had so lately been flushed with earthly passion and longing, now pale with starlight, enraptured, enamoured of the ideal. The silver light slept upon the white ceiling; the full effulgence of the moon swam in and found him still there. At length, with a sigh of bliss and satiety, faintly echoed by a vibration from the instrument, his head sank forward, and he lay at rest. Nothing sounded now save the deeper, more hidden harmonies of sky and river, seeking one another's voices – by day inaudible. The moon and stars sank and disappeared in turn, only the river flowed its appointed way, and the dawn came up, young, with a smile upon it...

Spring's touch was everywhere – in the air, on people's faces. Trees and houses, women and children, everything that could had donned its freshest apparel. The delicious sense of all-pervading, rapidly fleeting youth was astir that comes home to one nowhere more poignantly than in London, with its sharply defined contrasts of age and squalor, youth and beauty. Days of this bewildering charm seem even more absolutely ideal in grimy London than elsewhere. Yet an instinct is at work driving one forth to seek fresh fields.

On one such day it came about that the brother and sister from the Old River House, Dick Shadwell, and certain of their new friends, who were his old ones, took the water at Windsor meaning to spend the day in the Clive-den Woods. Amongst them were Gwendolen Brook and a reluctant mother, who yielded when she heard who was to be of the party. Of late the Brooks had lost sight of Richard Shadwell, but they valued his acquaintance, and were not sorry to have come upon him again. He was related to other and more valuable people than the Greys. Mrs Brook now tolerated even the Greys themselves, comfortably enough. She was getting used to her daughter's new and seemingly whimsical departures; in the long run she found they often turned out better than might have been expected.

It was long since the girl had consented to join the Greys in some such expedition, but, in the rush of days, the thing had been again and again put off till Leonard feared it was never to come to pass. His certainty about his own feelings and his uncertainty with regard to hers had produced in him an enervated and unnatural state of mind. He continued to work at his profession, but in a somewhat irregular fashion. It was difficult to keep up his old habits now that, for reasons of his own, he had, to some extent, cast in his lot with the world. To do work which shall have in it body and sinew, yet be at the same time ever so little 'the fashion' was, he found, no easy task.

Yet night after night, on his return from mundane gaieties, whither he went with the tacit understanding of reward in the shape of word or glimpse of Gwendolen, the pianoforte thrilled and trembled to his touch. But not now did it seem on the point of yielding up its heart to the player as it had done on a bygone night. Rather was it as its spirit shuddered and withdrew at his touch, though still at times he seemed to fancy he detected the baffling and alluring tones that whispered of fulfilment. Fevered, restless, wretched as he often was, a wild dawn of joy – the false dawn that perishes – would arise in his heart. His most cherished hopes were now, however, not in unison with the art to which he had once undividedly belonged. They were outside; centred in Gwendolen Brook and everything that concerned her.

The mere exercise of his musical faculty had once been all in all to him. Questions of praise or blame, success or failure, had not greatly troubled him. He had not even asked himself whether or no he had genius. Now all was changed. His new acquaintances were not troubled with over-reticence. Those especially least likely to recognise it if they saw it defined the quality of genius in a glib and facile manner, and unhesitatingly credited him with its possession. They told him such things in the spirit in which they told one another many a pleasant legend, not meant to be taken too seriously. But a young man, unaccustomed to the utterances of 'airy tongues', and especially anxious just then to believe in himself and his future, took them very literally. He heard, believed, and rejoiced greatly, instead of working out his own artistic salvation with fear and trembling. Avis, who had much of his own understanding and love of music, but who could not have defined genius as these men and women did, believed he had it. Was she right? Did she also rightly gauge the wild, ill-regulated character of his imagination, and the weakness of his will, and judge justly when she feared he was wandering in unsafe paths? His blind and uncertain happiness often became his bane, and then her silent companionship was the only thing that soothed and kept him in bounds.

His was a direct, simple and utterly uncomplex nature. He looked upon happiness as his right, and so long as there was reasonable prospect of securing it, so long as physical or mental enjoyment were attainable, he could struggle – but to fight a losing battle was not in him. When he could no longer bear the sound of the pianoforte that seemed at times to rise against him, complaining like a murdered spirit, or no longer promised the solution of its mystery or revealed the beauty and harmony of the outer world, but merely echoed his own restless longings, Avis alone kept him from plunging into wild folly or wilder despair.

So much is said and written about the preciousness of individuality, the beauty, duty, nay, the sacredness of living out to the full one's own nature – small or great – that unreasoning devotion and wholesale surrender like Avis Grey's are becoming rare, even among women. Her own fate and personality were irretrievably bound up with her brother's; she was contented, willing it should be so; how willing she did not realise, for she had never sounded the depths of her feelings and formulated affections. She was younger than Leonard, but to tend and cherish him, to watch his life and destiny unfold, as though she had, of her own, neither interests nor future, were her chief occupation and amusement.

Had she but known it, no story is more common than his. He wanted, he always had wanted, more than earth can give; his longing for material things, for every form of beauty and gladness, was only the unconscious craving after the ideal which had ever haunted him. What he longed for now was a star from the firmament, which wore a woman's form, a woman who smiled and shone on all alike, but who, through idleness or wantonness seemed to be shining for him alone. Such a story is common enough, but the joy and sorrow of it are as new to each one who figures in it as though they had not glanced over others' shoulders at its unfolding pages...

It was pleasant upon the river. Even the mother of Gwendolen felt its softening influence and experienced a sense of peaceful irresponsibility not usual with her. There is no better isolator than a river if we only suffer it to bear us away on its oblivious tide. Nothing carries us so far from the worries and cares of life, nothing so soon disperses unwelcome thoughts. The most careful and troubled spirits lose something of their burden drifting on a river's breast to the quiet haven where they would, but never could be, save for its gentle conveyancing. In her heart, too, Mrs Brook felt that her daughter might be trusted to do nothing 'foolish'.

'I hardly know why we are here, Mr Shadwell, except that Gwendolen would have it so,' she remarked. 'She was sure it would do me good, and I really *do* feel refreshed, and rested already.'

Mrs Brook was not a resting nor a restful sort of woman. She always wore some fluttering and quivering thing at her throat, and she generally had a scheme of some kind on hand, in which she was sure to involve people of an unguarded habit. In town or country she seemed ever speeding on the Primrose, or, it might be, some other path of usefulness or adventure. But she loved her daughter, ambitiously yet fondly, and she liked to see her enjoy her *menus plaisirs*, confident that she was wise enough in her generation not to allow them to interfere with serious aims. She was sure that no onlooker of responsible judgment, who knew Gwendolen and Leonard Grey and their respective positions, could possibly regard him in the light of a 'serious aim'. 'A right judgment in all things' was not amongst the young man's ideals, and how he might look upon himself, no one took into consideration.

Gwendolen appeared to be enjoying herself thoroughly, with that air of heart-whole enjoyment which helped to endear her to her family and acquaintance. Whether she took an oar, or steered with white, efficient fingers, or reclined in the stern, talking herself and making others talk, what she did was well and gracefully done. Yet she was not at ease. Leonard's passion for her was growing inconveniently importunate; what it must be to his own peace of mind her vain but not altogether unkindly nature forbore to consider. The dangers of playing Egeria to a man of his temperament, who knew little and cared less for the finer motives and methods of society, were becoming more manifest at each meeting.

She did him the justice to remember that 'for a man of his sort', as she mentally and mysteriously expressed it, he had been wonderfully patient; but she knew that the state of things could not last. She had found herself in such predicaments before now, and knew her ground. One way or another, she feared she must put an end to the situation, agreeable as in some ways it had been. It was a process she would fain have averted. Yet one day as well as another would do to make a beginning, or end, as it might prove, in spite of skill and judgment. She talked to him, therefore, apparently as before, but with a subtle difference. It was in a more abstract vein, and included Dick Shadwell or someone else nearly all the time. Dick remembered of old the gay, challenging, half-veiled mockery of her tone, as she took him to task with less than her usual tact as to life in general, and his own in particular. It was 'such a pity he should have placed himself outside the movement'. There was really so much going on that would interest him, if he would only condescend to be interested in the march of events. Surely he owed a duty to society, if not to his own individual friends! Shadwell was amused that she should take it so completely for granted that he had become a recluse, just because it had suited him to slip out of her own small kingdom. But he let it pass, and she went on –

'I only hope your influence may not have a sinister effect on your cousin's career, too, Mr Shadwell. You are not to teach him to 'burrow', as you have taken to doing! Mr Grey and his music have a distinct mission. It must be their task to wake the West End people up to a still deeper sense of their artistic darkness.'

She talked on, seemingly at random, but Dick knew that even as she chatted to him she was considering how she might best talk *at* Leonard. He understood her so well, her tones, her glances – he had had his opportunity – and he judged them and her with a very different judgment from his cousin's. With every utterance she managed to convey to the one most concerned the impression that he was making some sort of mistake about her; what he did not yet realise. He realised enough, however, to throw him off his balance, and to make the long looked-for day, a day of extreme wretchedness to him. As other women who play with fire have done before, she was anxious to lessen the force and fierceness of his attachment, yet to retain his worship. She did the thing well, but not well enough; the subject was not an easy one.

Avis, the while, her enjoyment marred by an uncertain sense that all was not well with Leonard, sat gazing on the changing, vanishing prospect, making little or no effort at conversation. Dick Shadwell looked at her from time to time, wondering a little at himself for the fanciful thoughts he had one day conceived concerning her. She looked sober enough just then to dispel a phalanx of such. But she interested him all the same; she was so entirely unlike any one but herself. He seldom spoke much to her, but he always felt her presence. Today she appeared as unconscious of his observation as usual. The passing sights and sounds seemed to claim her attention. Or was she, he reflected, away in one of her daydreams, concerning Leonard, his music, or his future?

The scenes they passed through were well known to Shadwell, and they looked to him less like realities than a series of bright and captivating sketches. The shining meadows, rich in buttercups; the cows stealing down them to water in the cool shallows beneath the giant trees; blue sky and fleecy clouds high and clear above them; the great bouquets of trees, their elegance of form not yet lost in masses of monotonous green, pleased his eye. How often he had seen the thing before here and on the walls of galleries, but custom did not destroy the charm. His artistic sense was cultivated rather than strong; and his misfortunes had not prevented him from developing his tastes. If there was less glory of untempered sunshine, there was, he thought, more glamour in the atmosphere, more play of sun and shadow. The few people they met had a value of their own; their voices, the splash of their oars sounded musical; their presence gave just the note of human brightness the landscape needed—no more. Later in the year how different it would be! A crowded highway is not so obnoxious as a crowded and jostling waterway, where a mob of people take their pleasure more or less violently; boats running into one another or the bank, angry and jocular comments flying; all the quiet nooks invaded, not, as now, with green shadow and silence, but loud with riotous colours and voices. Ah, no! when summer is young, or when she has died into autumn, and 'pleasurers' are few and far between, then is the time to learn the magic of the river as it shows itself on its higher banks!

Shadwell made sundry of these reflections aloud, and Mrs Brook and Gwendolen professed to find them both 'luminous' and entertaining. The beauty of the scene was, however, a good deal lost on Gwendolen; she was thinking about something else all the time, but she said appropriate things now and then, and said them well. Wandering by the river, pacing the terraces of the bright and deserted hotel gardens, it took most of her time and skill to stave off what she began to fear must be the inevitable expression of Leonard Grey's feelings. She was sincerely anxious to spare herself and him the ordeal, but to fence for ever with a person determined to come to an issue is impossible.

At evening in the quiet of the woods the pent-up feeling burst out. They were sauntering four abreast along a winding wood-way when the path narrowed, and somehow, by accident or design, Shadwell and Avis took the lead. To Gwendolen's annoyance, though she had too much pride to show it, they turned in another direction and disappeared.

'The woods are so sweet and pensive towards evening, and this stillness, how I delight in it!' she cried; 'but see, Mr Grey, we have lost the others, they have quite gone.'

'Let them go,' said the young man, bluntly, and rather gloomily. He had been waiting for some such moment; now it had come he feared a reverse. 'Let them go,' he repeated, and the fire leapt into his voice again as he went on. 'All day I have longed to speak to you. All day! It is months and months since I have wanted to speak. Oh, Gwendolen, I have longed to tell you something. You will, you must let me speak now.'

His voice broke a little, and he murmured something inaudible. She did not answer, and for a minute silence fell between them. The birds that had all day long 'filled the sky and air with their sweet jargoning' were mute, save a grieving thrush near at hand, who poured out its flood of song, then waited as though for an answer. The rare scent of green and growing life made itself felt in the stillness, the river rushed noiselessly by, the slender treetops were motionless against the sky. Love's hour had come; time, place, all was fitting, save the heart that would not, or could not, answer its call.

Standing at bay in the stillness near the man with whose happiness she had skilfully tampered, a vague sorrow, rather than remorse, a sorrow as for something lost or missed, surprised her. She thought of saying something, of 'rallying' him on his sudden silence, perhaps, but, looking at his set face, thought better of her intention, constrained at length to abandon her small subterfuges as unworthy of herself and him. But the silence began to press upon her; it seemed worse now than any speech could be. And still he paused, while to her something whispered that set her wishing she could love him as some women love men; enough to leave everything for their sakes. Even then she knew herself too well to believe in anything so impossible.

Then he spoke, and the softer instinct passed. She caught herself wondering why he should look so passion-tortured, so wild of speech and mien; and yet his expression showed how more than ready he was to believe in joy equally wild at a word or glance from her. It was not thus she dreamed of love, not thus it presented itself to her mind; if she allowed herself to picture it at all, it was as something far different. Yet in her heart she acknowledged its presence, even regretted its waste. An unknown want in her own nature seemed suddenly revealed by a lightning flash from his. Standing there before him, she felt herself growing small and cold and curiously poverty-stricken.

Vividly, suddenly, she realised that she had all her life been masquerading with feelings and emotions. Self-culture, East End charity, friendship, love, she had been playing with them all in turn, less from insincerity than from shallowness of nature. And now, when the reality of one of these sentiments was offered, she had only counterfeit coin with which to repay it. At the moment she came near a feeling like dislike and contempt of herself, almost of him for his worship. Then she braced herself to listen to the quick alternations of emotion that swept by her like a hurricane, or whispered with angel softness at her ear. In all she discovered no trace of the self-restraint and dignity of which she had heard and read, which she conceived to be 'the fitting birthright of every true Englishman'. Yet she passed through real emotions, pity, almost fear, but with an absence of comprehension, and a lurking distaste besides.

Long they remained in the darkening woodways, she chafing against the imprisonment, yet attempting – as became the *rôle* she had marked out for herself – quite unsuccessful reasoning and consolation, till she felt physically weary as after the buffetings of a severe storm. If this was the artist nature whose promptings she had thought she understood and might direct, how woefully had she mistaken herself and it! Now that she saw it in action it seemed violent and ill-regulated, the very nature most opposed to her own inmost idiosyncrasies. And yet that gentle regret – already she hoped in a dull way it might never become keen and gnawing – a regret as for something that had come and passed her by for ever, would mix itself alike with her pity and her shrinking!

At length it was over. He had made an end of speaking, but it was only to turn on her a long and searching gaze full of reproach and madness; to be met with an expression of cold and patient weariness which smote his pride, as well as his love to the quick. He made no more effort to detain her, and together they turned to reach the boats. The thrush had ceased its ineffectual song, the sunset pageant was passed, the tender colours had left the sky; already the clouds were like inky banners fringed with tarnished gold. The river lay very pale at their feet, all the charm washed out of it. The people in the boats, impatient to be gone, called to them to hasten, and their voices sounded thin and clear in the vast and gathering gloom.

## Some Pictures and A Portrait

'GOOD morning, Aunt Susan,' Dick Shadwell exclaimed, entering Mrs Grey's drawing- room, on a fine June morning, about midday. 'Good morning, Richard,' responded his aunt, mournfully, in return to his cheerful salutation. Shadwell had 'just looked in' on his way to the quiet club he still occasionally frequented. Mrs Grey had but now emerged from her own room. Her large armchair was wheeled forward to the window under the cool shade of the sun-blinds; everything she could require was placed ready to her hand by her daughter's watchful care. In her lap lay last year's copy of the 'Gardener's Chronicle'. It was large but light to hold, and she used it as a protection from conversational advances rather than with a view to horticultural research.

'And where are Leonard and Avis this lovely morning?' her nephew continued, still cheerfully. He sometimes adopted a rather provoking way of pretending to ignore his aunt's dislike to conversation, and her want of knowledge about her own family and household. In spite of constant and contrary evidence he continued to take for granted her interest in events connected with them. If it annoyed her – and he knew it did – the annoyance would do her no harm, he reflected!

'I wonder where they are,' he now continued; 'Where Leonard is. He hasn't been to see me for some time.'

'I am sure I couldn't tell you. You are more likely to know where he is than I am.'

Mrs Grey was goaded to reply at greater length than usual; and he felt he was getting on. For her part she wished her nephew was not so fond of asking useless questions; otherwise she had no fault to find with him.

'I want to take Avis a turn through the galleries. I don't think she's been, and I daresay she'd like it. Don't you think so?' he resumed, still glad to have made an impression.

'I can't tell, indeed. I daresay she would rather be quiet,' was the discouraging reply Mrs Grey was making just as her daughter re-entered the room. 'I want you to come and look at the pictures this morning. Will you, Avis?' he asked.

The girl hesitated a moment – not for permission from her mother, he knew she had not thought of it, and Mrs Grey had already interposed the Chronicle between herself and the world. It was of someone else she was thinking.

'If Leonard does not want me,' she began, tentatively and half irresolutely. 'He said he should be in the study all this morning, and he works better alone now; but a moment after he said he might go to Richmond, perhaps; …he may want me, you see. I'll find out.'

Shadwell took up a book, but he only looked at the outside, and put it down again absently. Mrs Grey was entrenched behind her screen, and appeared to be reading; but Dick guessed her thoughts were drifting elsewhere. Nothing daunted, he once more attacked her.

'Leonard seems a good deal changed just lately, don't you think so, Aunt Susan?' he demanded. She turned to look at him, repeating his words.

'Changed? I don't know, I'm sure. I daresay he is. I don't see much of Leonard. Perhaps he is busy; his music, I suppose. I don't like music, Richard; I never did.' She spoke with considerably more energy and decision than usual. He thought he was going to get something more than usual out of her at length, but at that moment Avis came in again.

'I can go if you like, Dick. He doesn't want me.' There was not much sign of pleasure or girlish eagerness in her voice. He noted the absence and the falling inflection in her tones with the passing wish that she were a little less quiet and acquiescent; for a girl of her years to be so staid was unnatural. But who, he reflected, could expect any other demeanour in a creature brought up under the shadow of such a mother?

For all that he found her a pleasant companion. In spite of her reserve he had learned to read a little in her feelings. The tones of her sensitive voice told him she was disturbed by Leonard's constant caprices and changes of plan; not because of their inconvenience to herself, but because his behaviour showed he was restless and out of gear. Otherwise she seemed happier, more alive than usual.

They went to more than one gallery, looking at pictures here and there, desultorily, without any plan. Even so, they saw as much as they wanted – and more. At one show they came face to face with Gwendolen Brook's presentment hung well on the line. It was one of the portraits of the year, and there was a small crowd and some movement and stir about it; not so subdued and 'refined' as the stir he remembered round the girl herself on her first appearance in his aunt's drawing-room. It brought that day back vividly to his mind: his aunt and Gwendolen seated together in the window, Leonard's eyes following all her movements, Avis, too, at the old pianoforte, how she had watched their farewells reflected in the ancient mirror, above her head! He was sure she had had a presentiment of evil even then, and already evil of a sort had sprung from the acquaintance. Gwendolen had proved a baleful influence in the life of the brother she worshipped.

The cousins stood side by side, not speaking, looking at the portrait. It was an excellent likeness as well as a clever painting of a really beautiful woman. He acknowledged, ungrudgingly, that she was lovely; that her charm of feature and form had not been overrated. The painter had happened to select and reproduce the very attitude, the very expression she had worn when she took her leave of Leonard at the River House, promising a speedy return. It was not an easy expression to seize and register – part earnest, a shade wistful, yet with a touch of mockery lurking somewhere in the half-smile. A look so fleeting, made up of so many emotions, was certainly difficult to give, but the painter had managed it admirably, so admirably that Dick caught himself wondering if he, too, were one of the many who had suffered the thrall of the sitter. The whole thing was so impressively, so vividly 'conveyed' that he felt as though he were again gazing at the girl as she had been on that first appearance of hers, long ago.

He did not look at his companion. He guessed, somehow, that her lips were touched with that repressed tremulousness he knew, and had, before now, divined she wished him not to know. He felt, rather than saw, the faint colour that crept to her cheeks, and he knew it was the unwonted flush of resentment, not admiration.

'It is very like,' he said, after a considerable pause. It the only remark either made, as they stood aside to allow others to take their place.

Avis did not share her mother's dislike and distrust of every form of art. On the contrary, she liked to see pictures, to hear good music, though she seemed not to dream that it was in her power to do something towards beautifying and gladdening her own surroundings. She was quite content now to wander whither her cousin listed, making occasional remarks, even now and again asking questions.

'You should go about more, Avis; Leonard should take you oftener to places,' Dick remarked, when he saw that change of scene already appeared to be working on her for good. Then it came out, in a roundabout but quite matter-of-fact manner, that she feared her mother might miss her if she were often away.

'Not that she cares to have me actually with her very much,' she said, simply, and as though it were the most natural remark for a daughter to make. 'But she would not like me not to be by. She wants things sometimes, and mother doesn't care to speak to the servants, you know.'

She paused, while Dick silently ejaculated, 'What a shame. The woman must be a perfect brute.' But he knew the next instant it was not true. His aunt was not a brute; only a woman who has fallen heavily into a groove, and who remained in it unconscious of its selfishness – perhaps because there was no pleasure in it. 'I suppose I could not get any new ideas into her head now, if I tried till all was blue,' he reflected, and went back to pleasanter subjects.

As they were leaving the gallery they came upon Gwendolen Brook herself – not unaccompanied. Coming straight from the portrait he for a moment underwent a species of disillusionment. The real woman was not quite the woman of the picture. As he now saw her she seemed not to possess, or to have lost something of the glamour and radiance of the portrait. Her face was harder, less changing than the painted one; there was less softness and play of expression, and yet it looked restless and unsettled. He would have bowed and passed on without speaking, but she came forward to meet them with a smiling face.

'Oh, Mr Shadwell,' she laughed, with an affectation of exaggerated vanity and egotism that somehow became her, 'You have been studying my portrait very attentively, I know you have; and then you were just on the point of trying to pass me by without speaking. It is a bad sign, I am afraid; it is a *very* bad sign.'

'You must put it down to the bedazzlement of my eyesight, Miss Brook,' he replied in the same sort of tone. But the artificial brightness had gone out or her face and manner, and she did not seem to hear him. She made no rejoinder, except to take Avis's hand in hers and hold it an. instant, as though she felt, instead of awkwardness, only a sort of pleasure in the meeting. For the first time, so far as her cousin knew in the girl's life, she looked really angry, and quickly withdrew it. Then with a few more words the three separated.

After they had passed on, Shadwell turned his head. Gwendolen was talking to one of the men at her side, but half looking back at them, somewhat in the attitude of the portrait. The inscrutable expression the great painter had so successfully reproduced was on her face once more. He wondered if Leonard had seen her again, or her picture. He could no longer wonder at his infatuation, nor at other people's, now and in the past. She was a heartless woman, perhaps, but men – some men at least – can forgive a woman with an expression like hers till seventy times seven if need be. Being a woman, Avis showed herself of sterner metal. The flush continued in her cheek, and she held her head higher, though made no remark on the meeting. Dick thought the touch of anger became her; he liked her all the better for it. Under it or some other influence she grew still more animated and talkative; she even made a suggestion or two about their next step and their luncheon. Altogether. they passed almost a brilliant afternoon.

He would have welcomed more such. They seemed to brighten her existence a little as well as his, yet he felt he must not, for many reasons, claim such hours too often. If her mother and brother were unconsciously selfish, it was no reason why he should be so consciously. Suppose he ended by teaching her the charm of a separate identity, he could never teach her the further lesson of merging that identity in his own. At times it was a great temptation to him to take his fill of the seemingly innocent joys that cropped up in his maimed existence, but he resisted it. That his own life was broken and useless must not make him careless of the lives and fate of others. He must take heed to his actions, if not for his own sake, for the sake of another person.

The Greys continued his chief interest, however. He became more and more a member of their household, more and more an element in their isolated lives. Sometimes he would look at Avis wondering how long things would thus go with her. It seemed not possible she should always be the same, living for others, belonging to others, without thought of her own personality. He could not picture her as an old woman, as in any way different from she was now. Yet he knew this entirely self-forgetting, utterly self-neglecting career was one that the young only may lead, before they have learnt to measure life in its meaning and significance, before they are forced by circumstances to calculate its chances and changes.

Her patience and calmness struck him less as being beautiful than as peculiar and unlike anything else. He had never seen her really moved, really stirred. He wondered how she would bear a shock or any great excitement. That she missed her brother's intimate companionship more than appeared, he felt sure. Leonard was seldom with her nowadays, being in his study, not – Shadwell imagined – working so continually as was supposed, yet brooking no inquiry or interruption, even from him. Sometimes the young man would set off on long and apparently aimless wanderings at strange hours, far into the suburbs, sometimes further afield still, as he told them when he returned later than usual, tired out, and strangely silent.

One night he did not return at all. That evening Shadwell stayed late at the River House, hoping he would appear; but one o'clock came, and he set off reluctantly without having seen him. He could see that Avis was secretly agitated, though she contrived to conceal all appearance of perturbation. She was reading aloud that evening, and she went on as usual. She often read aloud now. Mrs Grey seemed to like it; at any rate she preferred it to other forms of speech. Every time the bell rang the reader started and paused an imperceptible moment before going on. From her tone of voice Dick felt certain that she did not always follow the sense of the book. Yet when, on leaving, he sought to reassure her about her brother, she hid him goodnight quietly enough making little of her anxiety. His aunt did not appear to take in the situation fully, he thought.

Next day he made his appearance earlier than usual. Leonard had not returned. Mrs Grey was not out of her room, but Avis was watering plants on the balcony with rather a weary air, when a knock came to the door. In an instant she leaned over to see who it was, and Dick thought she grew a shade paler. A man's voice asked for 'Miss Grey', and presently a heavy tread was heard mounting the stair. The girl leaned on the balcony as though for support, but she said not a word. Shadwell stepped out to meet whoever it might be to ask his business. To his relief he found the man was only come to gather a delayed subscription. He never forgot the look of suspense his cousin turned on him when he came back, the expression of gratitude that passed over her face when he told her what was wanted.

Almost immediately after Leonard himself arrived. He seemed sorry for the anxiety he had caused, though unconscious of its depth. He accounted for his absence by telling them that he had been walking over Leith Hill, had lost his way and his train, and been obliged to put up for the night at the village inn. Richard, thinking he looked worn, haggard, and rather absent-minded, forbore to upbraid him with the alarm he had created. Soon afterwards he himself left London for a short tour in the Karpathians, and it was weeks ere he saw the Greys again.

## Chelsea Gardens

A SENSE of universal 'peace before death', a great benediction – not human – brooded over the fast-yellowing trees in the old river gardens. There was not enough stir in the air to sway the leaves ever so lightly as they fell sheer to the earth. The long lime avenue, now nearly deserted, was settling down to twilight. The noise of life passed by, or came distant and muffled.

One by one the old red-coated pensioners dropped off to seek more cheerful quarters. The children who had come playing and chattering about the benches where their elders sought snatches of repose were gone. The elaborate arrangements for some great game that never quite comes off were over for that day. Just as the scheme arrives at working order, when preliminary disputes and parts are settled, a ruthless maid or cruel elder sister arrives, and the small people are whisked off to bed, in a way that reminds one of 'Life and her processes'.

On a bench beneath the trees Leonard and Avis Grey still lingered. They were very silent. The impetuous vitality of the young man had died away, or showed itself rarely. He made no objection now when the girl proposed they should wait till Dick Shadwell came to join them. Presently from under the trees along the deserted paths came – not yet Shadwell – but a little procession they both knew. Quickly it moved towards them, a voiceless band of charity orphans, their scanty white cloaks falling stiffly about their childish forms, no glad laughter of youth sounding from their ranks. They vanished as swiftly as they came, each turning her chill young glance on the brother and sister. To Leonard it was as though they asked a question with their eyes – the question he was now always putting to himself, 'To what end, what end?' The soft autumnal haze crept upwards and onwards, the great shadows piled themselves at the base of the distant trees, and spread over the lawny reaches, touching the hard outlines of the blocks of buildings, and effacing their trivial details with uncertain, tremulous fingers.

'Stay with us, Leonard – do stay a little longer?' pleaded Avis, later, as the young man, interrupting a somewhat forced argument he and Dick had been sustaining, made a movement as though to rise. 'Oh, by all means. I'll stay till doomsday if you please. One place is as good as another – *quite* as good.' His tone was jocular, yet with an undercurrent of dull but bitter defiance. Coming from anyone but Avis the frequency of these appeals would have irritated him, and driven him yet further from his family and surroundings. Coming from her they were tolerated, they even seemed to keep his bodily presence at hand, though his thoughts were far off.

Never, by word or sign, even to Avis did he allow that Gwendolen Brook had anything to do with the change, in him. She had passed out of their rives, but her influence remained behind. Could he have obliterated all remembrance of her from his thoughts as well as from his speech, he would have asked no more. He had not enough vague love sentiment about him to help him to tolerate her thrall. It was not in his nature to find in it a sad pleasure, a charm of grievous pain. But to annihilate in a moment what has been, for long, the growth and spring of one's daily life is impossible, or requires a reactive power not possessed by people of the Grey temperament. Leonard despaired and suffered with all the force of youth and an undisciplined nature. The world seemed to him an altered place, to have turned mouldering and brown, because he himself was changed. So absorbed was he in his own nightmare of pain, that he sometimes woke from it and looked about him in surprise to find from the faces of the people around him that they had not been in hell too.

In one respect he and his mother were alike, they had a weakness in common – neither of them knew how to bear pain. She by reason of her low vitality, he because of the exuberance of his. Once it set in they made no head against it. In each a moral spring was deficient or absent.

He went back, it is true, to his music with fierce concentration, but it was no longer the same to him. The intimate relations between them seemed dead, or dying. The worldling may, with more or less impunity, play at art. The converse does not hold of the artist; sooner or later his art revenges itself on him for the desertion. It was so with Leonard. He found another refuge in the illusions of opium.

Dick Shadwell had more and more identified his solitary life with theirs. He was anxious about his cousin's condition, and the effect of it on his mother and sister – the latter particularly. He no longer laughed at Grey's prepossession with regard to the pianoforte, likening him to Mark Twain's youthful hero whose forlorn ambition it was 'to make of the potato a climbing vine'. On the contrary, he would have welcomed any interest, however unpractical, save the one he had found. The outward change seemed to have come on Leonard very suddenly; it only showed that his nature had required but a touch to break it down. All the easy-going sweetness and geniality seemed to have gone out of his disposition; its unconscious perversity and selfishness were now uppermost. Shadwell felt his own hold on him weakening, and his sister Avis got scant return for the untiring care she lavished upon him. As for his mother, whatever influence she had once exerted had long since fallen into disuse.

Her children had never been able to rouse her from the apathy into which she had fallen since her husband's alienation. Always reserved and silent, she had allowed herself more and more to settle into a mental and physical torpor from which nothing stirred her for any time. She took scarce any exercise, mental or physical; the result was that her retributive nerves seemed to become at times like red-hot wires, and she suffered from an indescribable nervous irritation. But she never spoke, never complained of the symptoms that haunted and oppressed her.

Tedious, persistent images and recollections would crowd unbidden to her mind, quickening her into painful restlessness, which she tried in vain to abate by continually pacing her own room. Her children were accustomed to the habit; they thought it was only one of their mother's 'ways'. They knew little of other people and other households. They had no standard by which to judge her, even had they dreamed of so doing. In all her loneliness and obscure suffering, her want of influence and acquaintance with her children, her slipping away from her rightful place, in life, rarely troubled her.

Sometimes, indeed, at late morning in her solitary chamber – the April showers rife on her darkened windows, all creation stirring and growing around her – memory awoke, and recalled, remorsefully, a bygone scene of her listless girlhood. She knew that even then it had seemed a wearisome triviality, yet again and again it presented itself... An old garden with dead grey walls and a perpetual rain falling on the budding lilacs, an old house, grey too, from whose windows she had gazed with freshening disgust or sick neutrality – windows whose farthest glimpse was of brown fields rising to meet the heavy sky, against which the stout plough-horses stood out a moment, disappearing and reappearing regularly. And gazing on it, then as now, the longing to get out into the wind-haunted wilderness she knew lay beyond was but faint and futile. In spite of its persistence, she knew that the buzz of insects and the sense of full sunshine extinguished by the soft rain had been hardly missed or enjoyed, the features of that scene had never stirred her heartstrings, had only vaguely suggested wilder images and wider cravings. Yet now it repeated itself with alluring tenacity and nauseous sweetness, even with a regret and longing she knew full well the real circumstances had not power to call forth. There came upon her a morbid craving for its repetition, though she knew a languorous acquiescence would be the sole emotion, as it ever was at that time, as, to her, it ever would be of all time – till time should be no more. The real longings, the aspirations, and efforts, the years should have brought the affections and interests that should now be grown up about her, all joys in the present, all hopes in the future shut out, or turned to wrecks and perishing dreams, by the weary dripping of the rain on the new buds, in that old, old garden...

Her children might be kind, even affectionate, her nephew attentive and patient; but no heart could reach hers, no human hand soothe a trouble so deeply rooted and obscure, nor minister to a mind so diseased.

The young people in the gardens rose at length and turned reluctantly towards the River House. It should have been a pleasant and restful place, but had never been aught but sorrowful and shadowy to most of its dwellers. It looked quiet and very sombre when they reached it, the falling twilight as yet undispersed and undisturbed by lighting. Shadows loomed in the narrow overgrown garden, seeming to await their coming, and to follow in their wake, trooping up the wide staircase, as though the real owners – the others but shadows.

Avis, before joining Leonard in the study, passed to her mother's room to see if she appeared to want anything, if need were to read her to sleep. Richard Shadwell, cigarette in hand, turned to pace the dim garden. If Leonard should care to see him before he went to his rooms, near at hand, he would be on the spot.

'There they go,' he mused within himself, when the girl's slight figure had quite disappeared. 'There they go,' and he smiled, but not gaily, 'breaking their hearts and intellects over that monster.' He referred to the pianoforte, but Gwendolen Brook may have been in his thoughts as well. The minutes passed; he had paced the garden many times ere the sounds of music floated to him from the house.

Motionless, stretched in a long chair, Avis found her brother. There was no sign nor symptom that he had done any active work for some time. She had lost the habit of coming often to this room, for Leonard rarely now encouraged her visits. As she looked about at the chaos around her, something like despair came into her quiet eyes. Papers, endless, untidily arranged papers met her at every turn: everywhere papers and MS, (from which no good thing would any more come), stacked together on chairs, in odd corners, on the floor. The splashed inkstand and bottles were dry and dusty, the pens rusted in a heap. From the wreck and ruin about him she turned to the man himself. He had not stirred on her entrance, but she knew it was no natural slumber that held him. His fixed yet vacant gaze had been looking at other sights than these, ever changing visions not bound by four straight walls. The ineffable ecstasy, the unutterable agony was over, yet the limitless abysses, the boundless reaches, and awful silences of his dream scenery were still more real than his actual surroundings.

How long he had been thus wandering, untethered by space and time and his own sickening identity, he could not have told; he only knew he was once more 'coming back', the worst experience of those belonging to a diseased consciousness. The girl went nearer, with her usual staid and quiet tread. Then bending over the back of the chair, silent but uncontrollable tears, never shed for her own sake, suddenly gushed from her eyes and fell on his dark hair. Turning, he seemed to see or feel her weep. The sight was so strange and unexpected to him that for a moment dawning reason and wretchedness struggled helplessly in his eyes. Blessings and curses rose incoherently to his lips, then suddenly, in an impulse of pure love and pity for her alone – not for himself – he caught the little creature to his breast and wept in anguish…

Below in the garden Dick Shadwell had been waiting his summons or the familiar sounds of the pianoforte. He hoped that one demon of unrest might exorcise another, and help Avis in her soothing task. Even as he wished it she leaned to him from the staircase window to say goodnight, and to tell him she had left Leonard better, more like himself. But in her quiet, reserved voice he noted a jar, as of some fresh pain. Then, as though in confirmation of her words, the sound of music was borne out to him on the quiet air. At first it sounded like a resigned and solemn strain, the requiem of a hope, then gradually the sounds increased in force and volume. Dick could almost fancy he saw the musician labouring at the instrument with a sort of infernal power, it seemed to writhe and quiver beneath his touch as though he sought to wring from it the impossible, the unattainable. 'Ah,' thought the listener, 'he is as far, then, as ever from his hopes, from his solution; the kingdom of music is not thus taken by violence!'

Suddenly with a harsh crash the sounds ceased, and to his dismay were followed by a short, sharp explosion. With a presentiment of horror which told him what had happened, and that almost unconsciously to himself he had been expecting something like it, he ran up the garden and entered the drawing-room by the back way. He was swift, but someone else was swifter. At the side of Leonard, stretched motionless on the floor, a flood of light falling from the ceiling upon her, knelt Avis. No wringing of her hands, no cry came from her lips. She remained, motionless as though paralysed, with wide-open eyes that saw nothing, lifeless as her reflection in the polished wood of the pianoforte at her side, the pianoforte that seemed to take all so pitilessly, giving back – what? That other piano picture of long ago flashed incongruously on his mind. The hair, the brow, the self-same outline, all was there; only where the flowers had laid their crimson glow upon her breast a red stain instead – the red of death! How long did he stand thus aloof? In reality but a second, and then he was at their side with help that might avail the dead only – the living, what help of his or of anyone else might reach her?

## A Little Speech and Some Music

'IF a stream cannot flow one way it will another,' says an old Servian proverb. The brief tide of life and gaiety that had set to the River House took other directions. Summer and winter it was quiet enough now. Only the river went by as before; but from the windows no music or laughter sped it on its course. All the world over there are such places, graves of dead hopes, of old joy and laughter. Where do such things go? Has the impalpable its own shapes? Have fiery aspirations and tender whispers ghosts of their own, as well as the people who give such things birth? Let us hope the other world may not be like some vast phonograph, storing them up only to give them back clear, thin, and inhuman.

More like shadows than ever the women pursued their household ways. Outwardly Mrs Grey was least changed of the two, but Avis looked more and more unsubstantial. They exchanged no words about the dead son and brother. His loss and the manner of it was an ingrowing, increasing wound which external appliances, like speech and time could not heal or mitigate; The unbroken quiet the mother had once craved was deep enough now, and, like all else, it was hateful to her. The acquaintances her son had rapidly made had as rapidly dispersed. She desired none for herself, she seemed not to think that they, or any other interest, might be necessary to Avis; she appeared to note no change in her always grave and reserved demeanour.

Richard Shadwell alone remained to them. There are people who become, as it were, our daily bread, whose presence in our lives is scarcely recognised till it is withdrawn. Both women unquestioningly accepted his care and tenderness, making no return in the shape of confidence or seeming affection. He found them in every way, as he always had found them – unlike other women, and more negative than positive. So much so, that it was sometimes difficult to know how to take them. He tried to interest, to amuse them, even to shake them out of themselves; but their feelings lay too deep for that. It was not easy to appeal to them from any point of view. To sympathise with them openly was impossible, they were so dumb and speechless, so apt in hiding every glimpse of their sufferings or affections. They had not enough idea of the nature of social obligation to make the slightest pretence at a show of ordinary cheerfulness, for their own and others' sakes.

Had he been free, he wondered if he could have made Avis love him. There seemed a sort of sacrilege in the thought; as well ask a ghost to love one as the gentle, fragile girl. It sometimes struck him that it was no wonder if Leonard had sometimes felt in prison beside them. They had no pretty feminine softnesses; they never gave him a look of thanks, a caressing word, in all their days together. Yet they appealed to him with the force of their very forlornness. His former friends might have wondered could they have seen his tender care of these two impassive people.

Of the two, Avis was the one most devoid of recuperative power. She seemed to him the rare instance of a woman whose affections and faculties will work but in one direction; cut off the channel and life withers at the source. Her affections had, he thought, been entirely and irrevocably given to her brother; her intellect and imagination were centred in her music. Perhaps on her own account, perhaps on her mother's, she now shrank from touching what had been an influence in his life. Dick speculated as to how far this was her own or her mother's doing. He suspected it was Mrs Grey's grim touch that had shut, locked, and jealously shrouded the pianoforte. He wondered how they could so passively endure the sight of it, still in the old place, but beneath its white shroud. To him it looked eerie and suggestive of unpleasant ideas. At times, if a heavy footfall or movement jarred it, it vibrated to the sound; sometimes even at the light footstep of the girl he thought it trembled faintly, as though a sigh rose from its muffled heart.

Was it the sigh of a gentle prisoned spirit, or of a dogged force waiting the supreme touch which was one day to reveal it? This piece of mechanism, this block of wood and ivory, would outlive many more rash mortals than those who had dreamed of finding its secret, and now lay in closer, deeper darkness than enfolded it. As Dick had said, the atmosphere of the Old House certainly set him dreaming as he never did elsewhere. He imagined the keys of the piano as great teeth smiling beneath the shroud, a monstrous threatening smile at those who thought to master it. Did it really fear the touch that might give its secret to the world, or was it baffled hope and longing that stirred the poor monster at the sound of the frail girl's tread?

How its release from bondage came no one quite knew, nor who it was who removed the trappings. But one day, outside the drawing-room door, Shadwell stopped abruptly as an unwonted sound fell on his ear.

The pianoforte was at work again. Through the closed door soft music stole out to him where he stood, music that touched his heart as with a spell, so captivating a tale it told. It seemed to speak another language than it had done under Leonard's influence. It spoke – or so Dick then interpreted it – of the beauty, nay, the joy of grief, of the pale and radiant flowers that spring into blossom with each tear that falls on its arid soil, of that 'insight too deep for joy to measure' that comes of 'supremacy of pain'. As though his very being depended on hearing and understanding aright, the young man listened, and as he listened his face looked for the time transfigured.

On it pealed, ineffably sweet yet majestic, as though it scaled the heights and depths of time and eternity, as though by some magic the heart and soul of the instrument were at length laid bare. If someone were but at hand to take it down in writing, to register the sounds, had been his first thought; but that had soon faded, leaving no place for anything save the sounds themselves. All else was forgotten. Every faculty went out to follow their meaning and significance. They came to the listener like a revelation of some unknown path, untrodden and unvisited by human intelligence and experience. Like sound made visible, yet detached from everything material, it took intangible yet palpable form before the ears and eyes of his imagination. Soft, soft, then softer still, till it died away as something that has been and is not. A moment he paused, then, as though awakening from a many-coloured, vivid reverie, he turned to open the door.

In the attitude of one merely at rest, Avis Grey had sunk rather than fallen forward on the instrument. He thought her narrowly-prisoned spirit had already returned to the larger place whence it came – on the waves of her strange melody. Not a vibration remained to tell the story of her inner life, of this, her latest experience. Had Death and the pianoforte conquered, and were their secrets once more safe and intact?

Before the end came she spoke a few words, however – for her they seemed many. Richard Shadwell bent his head to listen, and she spoke in his ear –

'Are you there, Dick? – so very kind, *always*! I wish you were happier. I have always loved you, loved you and – him. My poor mother! Take care of her!'

What a new light those words cast on the past they had shared together! Even the future, that must be spent without her, seemed illumined beforehand.

## *Where The Dead Lie*

IN the crowded wilderness of the Brompton Cemetery there is a spot more sparsely tenanted. There the grass grows rank and bitter; one side is shut in by great mausoleums, their iron gateways barring the black nothingness within, or gaping sometimes as though to reveal a darkness even deeper. Often to this spot comes a woman, sometimes a man, and they sit awhile side by side, silent with folded hands. Nearby the living leave many a token for the dead, besides their prayers and tears – crosses, wreaths, flowers – immortal or perishing… These two bring themselves only; no rose or cypress marks the twin graves they so often seek. They exchange no words or memories; silently they come, and silently pass away. The sun shines, the rain falls on the mounds of the hopelessly still graveyard, and on these two as brightly and kindly as on the favoured ones where figures bend and passionately invoke the impossible uprising of the dust beneath. Yet who may say what these two remember, as they witness the hopes one man fled from and abandoned, conquered and perfected by those still in the strife, while he sleeps in his place, his gentle guardian at his side?

Later, it often struck Shadwell how logical was his companion's attitude, how characteristic of her whole life and bearing! The outward grace and beauty of life which the man she secretly but despairingly mourned had appreciated with all the strength of a sensuous nature had not been anything to her. Such things to her were meaningless, or worse, and she never pretended it was otherwise. She had not ministered to her children's desires and needs in life; in death she did not do so either. For Avis's sake, and for her own, Dick accompanied her on these visits, and gave up much of his life to hers.

He, too, had a visit to make, but she made no mention of it. It was a periodical visit to another part of London, and the person he went to see at times knew him – not always. Sometimes she only shuddered at the sight of him with a nameless, meaningless fear; at others she raved wildly, her wrecked beauty aflame with the fire of unquenchable madness. Mrs Grey never sought to know, never inquired if he found things better or worse, if he continued his visits. It was enough that he was at her side when she made her own.

Shadwell would not have expected, much less wished, to see her engage in any of the cheerful and elaborate gardening that went on in many parts of the city of the dead. He rather revolted than otherwise from the array of watering-pots, the hustling and bustling at the well, the active raking, scraping, and burrowing that went on over the fallen heads – the end well-nigh forgotten in the means. The remarks of the workers, 'obliging' one another, as they called it, with a tool or a bulb, and the acrimonious verbiage that sometimes resulted, were certainly distasteful to him. Yet, since his companion made a practice of coming, he would have understood in her the natural impulse just to stoop and remove a noxious weed. She never stretched out a finger. What she had been she remained, absolutely inactive in grief, as in all else. Here, and at home in the Old River House, she was to all appearance, unaltered. Sluggish and impassive she had been in her children's life, so she remained, so – he mused – she probably would remain till swept into the universal waste heap, where even habit loses its dread force; unless, as some think, the weight of custom only then begins in its full and awful power.

# 13
# Last Act

ONE APRIL AFTERNOON in 1939, a small group of family and friends followed the coffin of Katharine de Mattos to her lasting resting place in Edinburgh's New Calton Cemetery. Some 87 years after her birth in that city, Katharine's body was interred in the grated cell where three generations of Stevensons lay buried already, from the great lighthouse builder Robert onwards. Inside the mausoleum was a separate stone for her father and Aunt Alan, who had died in 1895 at the house in Chelsea. And in 1900 Katharine's parents had been joined there by her brother Bob, the brilliant talker whose artistic dreams remained unrealised when death came at 53. But Bob died in the knowledge that he was survived by a six-year-old son Thomas, who would marry and have three children, transmitting Bob's 'latent capability' to new generations.

Also at rest in the family vault lay Louis's father, the man after whom Bob had named his son. And a decade after Bob took his cousin's place at Tom Stevenson's funeral, the iron gates had been opened again for Aunt Maggie, who on returning from the South Seas had spend her last two years in her home city. Only their son was not there, for her 'darling Lou' had died suddenly on the verandah of his colonial home when a stroke robbed the world of its best-loved author at the age of 44. Louis now lay 'under the wide and starry sky' on a mountaintop in Samoa, his body accompanied to the grave by the many islanders who mourned his passing.

So, too, had Katharine mourned when the fateful 'Death of RLS' posters appeared on news stands across London on 18 December 1894, a fortnight after the event on the other side of the world. A silly quarrel may have alienated the cousins but she would never stop loving Louis. His place could not be taken by her other friends, however gifted they were, from the doomed, dark artist Aubrey Beardsley to the poet Alice Meynell or the painter James Abbott McNeill Whistler.

Yet as a master of horror Louis almost had his equal in Katharine's next-door neighbour in Chelsea. Just through the wall of her mother's house in St Leonard's Terrace, an Irish barrister and theatrical manager sat at his desk in a bright and pleasant room overlooking the back garden, spending seven years creating the masterpiece that would make his name immortal. Katharine, who had once met the son of Frankenstein's creator and was in at the sensational three-day birth of *Jekyll and Hyde*, lived also within touching distance of Bram Stoker's *Dracula*.

We do not know if the creator of vampires ever showed her the manuscript before publication in 1897, or if the link Katharine supplied between Mary Shelley, Stevenson and Stoker was any more than a geographical coincidence, but her friendship with HG Wells may have helped influence his early work. Her description of the laboratory experiment in which the sinister scientists liberate the spirit from the figure slumped in a chair in *Through The Red-Litten Windows* – 'A body had been made invisible, obliterated; a something, a spirit, had been set at large, liberated. I knew not; my strained vision relaxed, consciousness deserted me, and I lay back, free myself, for a space, of thought and time' – may have planted the seed from which Wells developed his description of the liberation of mind and body from time and space in *The Time Machine*: 'I pressed the lever over to its extreme position. The night came like the turning out of a lamp, and in another moment came to-morrow. The laboratory grew faint and hazy, then fainter and ever fainter. To-morrow night came black, then day again, night again, day again, faster and faster still. An eddying murmur filled my ears, and a strange, dumb confusedness descended on my mind.'

Yet Katharine's own literary endeavours met with little success beyond journalism. Critical reaction to *Through The Red-Litten Windows* and *The Old River House* had been lukewarm, although it was 'Theodor Hertz-Garten' not Katharine who took the blame. Unwin's newspaper advertisements for No 11 in its Pseudonym Library series used a curious quote from a *Scottish Leader* review – 'A remarkable short imagination' – plus one bald sentence from the *Observer*: 'The Old River House is well written, interesting, and full of artistic detail.'

*The Morning Post* reviewer wrote: '*Through The Red-Litten Windows* and *The Old River House* are two stories by Mr Theodor Hertz-Garten. The first is a weird tale prompted by the ravings of a disordered brain. It is sufficiently well written to induce the regret that the author should have employed his power on so thoroughly unwholesome a theme. *The Old River House* is also sad beyond the average, but here, at least, a series of moving, if somewhat vague, psychological pictures show a firm, yet tender touch.'

To be fair to Katharine it should be noted that in 1886 the *Morning Post's* reviewer had likewise failed to appreciate *Jekyll and Hyde*: 'Clever as Mr RL Stevenson has shown himself to be, it is doubtful whether his undeniable talent will suffice to render his new tale popular. On the surface it seems to be a weird and powerfully told sensation story. But as it develops itself it is found that its principal personage has a dual individuality, and that he can, at will, transform himself into quite another by drinking a potion invented by himself.'

The wholesome *Woman's Herald* gave a longer review to Katharine's little book but was less kind: 'This last publication of the Pseudonym Library is not as good as its predecessors. A flavour of ghosts and a soupçon of crime is not enough to satisfy our mental palate. In *Through The Red-Litten Windows*, we have a hasty hysterical young man who has quarrelled with his brother-in-law and has exiled himself from home, and respectability. In an excited state of mind he betakes himself to Regent's Park and while wandering about in the dark is accosted by a lovely lady under whose magnetic influence he forgets all laws of common sense and the natural love of self-preservation, and submits to be a passive witness of a series of mysterious incidents which point to crime, but are never satisfactorily explained. The end of this feeble young man is as unsatisfactory as his conduct throughout.

'The other tale, *The Old River House*, is somewhat better written, though again the author deals only with characters whose mental mechanism is strung to the pitch of madness. One looks in vain for anything bright, or natural, or healthy, in page after page of dreary morbidity, and impressive gloom. The writer has wasted his talent on such unpleasant subjects. There is no lesson to be learned, no improvement to be gained from reading of melancholy maniacs who pervert God's gifts and wilfully shut their eyes to the light that everywhere surrounds them.'

Yet Katharine's weird, unhealthy tales of melancholy maniacs were paralleled in real life by the unsavoury antics of her estranged husband. Shortly after her book was published, complaints reached the Fabian headquarters that Sydney de Mattos was greatly harming the society by his moral position on free love and by gossip involving a female lecturer whose lecture tours he organised.

Kate St John Conway, a Cambridge-educated bluestocking, had been so impressed by the cause of striking cotton workers in Bristol that she left her job at a private school for girls to teach in a state school, lodging with a working-class socialist family. De Mattos arranged for her to give a series of lectures in the provinces, arranging her accommodation and generally looking after her needs on tour. Unfortunately it seems he made sexual advances and tongues wagged. Miss Conway was forced to tell the general secretary she could no longer work with him and the summer programme of lectures was cancelled.

George Bernard Shaw was well aware of his fellow Fabian's sexual incontinence, describing him as a 'satyromaniac', but seemed to take a humorous view of it. In the summer of 1892, de Mattos was arranging lectures in Oxford, where a leading light of the branch was one William Hines, a sweep employed to keep the many college chimneys clean. Hines lived with his wife Mary in St Clement Street, with a son and eight daughters squeezed into one little house. The daughters were well educated, with a least two of them working as teachers while another became a herbalist, but they were not ready for the likes of de Mattos.

In August 1892, Shaw wrote in a letter: 'I hear from Oxford that de Mattos is ravishing every maiden in the country, and that even the tolerant Hines took umbrage when some seven or eight of his daughters had succumbed.' If this is not an exaggeration, de Mattos with his gospel of free love seduced Rebecca, 27, Minnie, 26, Emily, 24, Ann, 21, Ada, 19, Kate, 16, and maybe 14-year-old Flora or even 12-year-old May. With the age of consent raised from 13 to 16 some seven years previously, Katharine's estranged husband was starting to look like a sex criminal.

Yet despite his unfortunate reputation de Mattos got on well with his fellow Fabians and in 1893 he and George Bernard Shaw went up to Bradford to the conference at which the National Independent Labour Party was founded. The working-class socialists were initially suspicious of the two Fabians who had to observe the meeting from the gallery until, by a narrow vote, de Mattos and Shaw were permitted to take part. Sexual impropriety aside, the man who could not be trusted with his own wife's marriage settlement was made a trustee of the large legacy left by the millionaire and Fabian supporter Henry Hunt Hutchinson to further the socialist cause.

But the Fabian career of de Mattos would not last much longer, for in 1898 he departed suddenly for Canada. Was this to escape the consequences of free love, or was he simply hard up without access to his wife's marriage trust and hoping to strike lucky in the Klondike gold rush? His two children remained in England. Richard, now 21, had spent much of his childhood at boarding school while his mother kept working for *The Athenaeum* to pay the fees. Now a Catholic, and as if to atone for his Godless father's sexual improprieties, Richard had decided to become a monk in a Franciscan community in Wales.

Until the age of 26, Snoodie lived with her mother. On the death of Aunt Alan, she and Katharine shared a flat in Albany Mansions, Battersea until 1902, when Snoodie married Frederick Dalton and the couple moved north, living in Coventry, Loughborough and the small town of Mirfield in Yorkshire. Eventually they would have four sons and emigrate to Canada, settling in Vancouver. As Sidney de Mattos was in British Columbia, now living in Prince George in the Cariboo gold-mining district, Snoodie may have been reunited with her father, who remained legally married to her mother until his death in 1929.

With the departure of Snoodie, Katharine lived alone. *The Athenaeum* continued to pay well, and while her own literary career had stalled she had been generous in support of other talents. She was one of the few who championed the cause of Aubrey Beardsley when his distinctive illustrations for Oscar Wilde's *Salome* appeared in 1894 to public uproar and accusations of depravity. Beardsley's pictures of coldly beautiful, sexually empowered women might equally well have been the mysterious *femme fatale* who destroys the young man in Katharine's *Red-Litten Windows*.

Beardsley would be dead himself before his 26th birthday in 1898, his final struggle against consumption played out in Menton where Louis had sought health 25 years previously. But Beardsley did Katharine one small favour in return for her kindness. As co-founder and illustrator of *The Yellow Book*, the leading literary and artistic journal of *fin de siècle* Britain, he wanted to include an example of her work alongside the likes of Max Beerbohm, Arnold Bennet, HG Wells and WB Yeats. Beardsley persuaded Yellow Book editor Henry Harland to include one of Katharine's poems, despite the objections of the magazine's publisher John Lane. In a letter to Lane, Harland said it was 'a poem which you don't like, but which Beardsley and I like very much: besides she is the first cousin of Robert Louis Stevenson, and the sister of R.A.M.S., the *Pall Mall* critic'. And so Katharine, despite refusing to trade on her cousin's famous name, was granted a grain of literary immortality on the strength of his reputation, and that of her brother:

## In A Gallery: Portrait of A Lady (Unknown)

Veiled eyes, yet quick to meet one glance
Not his, not yours, but *mine*,
Lips that are fain to stir and breathe
Dead joys (not love nor wine):
Tis not in *you* the secret lurks
That makes men pause and pass!

Did unseen magic flow from you
Long since to madden hearts,
And those who loathed remain to pray
And work their dolorous parts –
To seek your riddle, dread or sweet,
And find it in the grave?

Till some one painted you one day,
Perchance to ease his soul,
And set you here to weave your spells
While time and silence roll;
And you were hungry for the hour
When one should understand?

Your jewelled fingers writhe and gleam
From out your sombre vest;
Am I the first of those who gaze,
Who may their meaning guess,
Yet dare not whisper lest the words
Pale even painted cheeks?

Yet fame in *The Yellow Book* did not lead to greater things, and for the rest of her career Katharine would content herself with reviewing 'novels of the week'. Aside from her literary acquaintances, her closest friend was poor Walter Ferrier's sister Coggie, with whom she could share private memories of Louis. Bob had been Katharine's mainstay, and without her weekly visits to see him in Chiswick she felt bereft. She kept in touch with Louisa until her death in 1909, and thereafter with Bob and Louisa's daughter Margaret, who inherited the family home and eked out a living in Chiswick as an artist's model, remaining unmarried until her death at 41. There may also have been occasional meetings with Margaret's brother Thomas, his wife Emma and their young brood to brighten Katharine's day.

There was also Katharine's sister Dora. The path of matrimony had not run smooth for any of the three Stevenson sisters. Mab, having survived the unpleasantness of marriage to Alec Gibson Thomson, found new happiness with her second husband in Africa – but like Bob she would not make old bones, dying in Lagos at the age of 51. Yet it was Dora who had the worst experience of marriage, to a loveless brute who abused her while fathering five children. Richardson Fowke had been a spoilt young man until the family finances ran out, obliging him to work as an office boy before becoming a teacher. After a brief career as a classics master, he departed with his brother to run a coffee plantation at Dickoya in Ceylon.

In 1876, on a trip back to Europe, he met and married Dora Stevenson. When the newlyweds boarded the liner for Ceylon, poor Dora had no idea of the hell in store for her when her husband's Mr Hyde side was revealed. What Fowke had not told her was that he had a wife already in Dickoya. In 1873 he had married Mary Bird, who gave birth to their daughter Ruth in 1874 and a short-lived son Henry in 1876 – three months after her husband's bigamous marriage to Dora. For the next three years in Ceylon, Fowke had two wives – and if either of them discovered they were part of a squalid *menage à trois,* they should have known not to complain, for Fowke was a violent, abusive husband. When Mary died suddenly in 1879, it was rumoured he had killed her.

'Big Dora', as she was known in the Stevenson family, was perhaps more able physically and temperamentally to absorb the abuse over the years in which Fowke fathered five children, two girls and three boys, and ill-treated them, too. They were all terrified of their father. When his plan to make their eldest daughter Katherine marry a Ceylonese man led to her attempting suicide and fleeing to the Nigharry Hills with her mother, Fowke then forced her to marry a German at two days notice. Fowke's treatment of his sons was equally monstrous, eventually abandoning them at boarding school in England without paying the fees, and one of them was so traumatised that his mental development was impaired for life.

Dora herself was a large, placid woman with a vague temperament that distanced her from her surroundings, rather like Mrs Grey in *The Old River House*. It enabled her to withstand life with her husband until her 5th pregnancy. Then she fled Ceylon for England and sought refuge with her mother and Katharine in Chelsea, where the baby was born in 1888. In that year *A Book of Verses* by WE Henley was published, including a pen portrait of Dora, possibly at Margate and already pregnant with her son Rohan:

*Back-View*
To D.F.

I watched you saunter down the sand:
Serene and large, the golden weather
Flowed radiant round your peacock feather,
And glistened from your jewelled hand.
Your tawny hair, turned strand on strand
And bound with blue ribands together,
Streaked the rough tartan, green like heather,
That round your lissome shoulder spanned.
Your grace was quick my sense to seize:
The quaint looped hat, the twisted tresses,
The close-drawn scarf, and under these
The flowing, flapping draperies—
My thought an outline still caresses,
Enchanting, comic, Japanese!

This was written before Katharine's showdown with Henley, from which their friendship never recovered. Henley, having suffered the tragedy and guilt of losing his little daughter at the age of five from tuberculosis inherited from her father, then launched a posthumous attack on his old friend in a scathing review of Graham Balfour's *Life of Robert Louis Stevenson*. The original Long John Silver scandalised the world of Stevenson worshippers by decrying the book's portrayal of the *Jekyll and Hyde* author as 'this Seraph in chocolate, this barley-sugar effigy of a real man'. And Katharine, who still carried a candle for her cousin and knew the reason for Henley's spleen, was appalled like the rest, including Fanny Stevenson, now recovered from her mental health problems.

Fanny had once claimed Katharine as a friend, but for a long time they were estranged by the Nixie quarrel, with Katharine in her flat in Battersea and Fanny in San Francisco, in a grand house built with her late husband's royalties. More than a decade after Louis's death they met again when Fanny took a holiday in England, and it seems there was some kind of reconciliation before Fanny's death in 1914. The two women had much in common. Both were fiercely independent, intelligent and literary, yet cursed with unfaithful husbands. Katharine's was now away in Canada, but what of Sam Osbourne? Did the pile of clothes on a Californian beach belong to a man who drowned – or emerged on the other side of the world to continue his philandering?

In 1896, the San Francisco journalist Barbour T Lathrop was in South Africa, where he bumped into Sam Osbourne in Johannesburg. Yet on greeting the man he had known for eight years at the Bohemian Club and the San Francisco law courts, Lathrop was blanked by Fanny's former husband, who responded: 'You are mistaken, my name is not Osbourne.' Clearly he did not wish to be recognised, for reasons best known to himself. 'All right, Sam,' said Lathrop. 'If you want to go masquerading under another name, it is none of my business. Good day, sir.'

In London, Big Dora was living in straitened circumstances with her daughter, also called Dora, in Chiswick – a mile from Bob's daughter Margaret, who may have given 'Little Dora' the idea of working as an artist's model to eke out their small income. Dora, Katharine and Bob had all benefited from Louis's will. Despite Fanny's opposition, their estranged cousin had honoured his promise to his father to leave a quarter of Tom Stevenson's estate to the three of them. It was not much, but it would have helped Dora and Margaret keep the wolf from the door – and to cushion the blow when Katharine's work for *The Athenaeum* dried up in 1908.

At 57, she may have fallen out of fashion or simply decided it was time to retire and live 'on her own means', such as they were. She did not see much of Richard – when he finally turned up on her doorstep after years shut away in a monastery, the servants did not recognise him, and he then went on to be a Catholic priest. But until Snoodie and her family departed for Canada, Katharine could still visit them up north and enjoy her grandchildren. Meanwhile in London she kept an eye on Dora, on her own since Little Dora's departure to India to marry the advocate general of Madras. The brutal Fowke had expired in Paris in 1899, two years after being prosecuted for a second crime of bigamy. While still married to Dora, he feloniously wed Astrid Dahl Benson at Kensington Register Office. Denying the offence, he was sent for trial and convicted, whereupon Dora finally divorced him.

Dora's death in 1931 saw Katharine increasingly isolated and succumbing to dementia. When the end came in 1939, the *Times* obituarist glossed over her rift with Louis: 'She never spoke of the Henley-Stevenson quarrel, over some writings of hers, which Fanny Stevenson published under her own name. She was essentially unselfish and remained friends with both sides. The shadows began to close in a few years ago; her memory became impaired; her brilliant charm and conversation failed. It was good that God took her, for she outlived her friends and her intelligence.'

To the end, Katharine had avoided talking of her famous cousin in public. The one exception was in 1922, when at the age of 71 she made a guarded contribution to a book of reminiscences called *I Can Remember Robert Louis Stevenson*, protesting: 'I am always a little loath to write of intimate friends and personal matters. But as you so kindly invite me to say what I can of my great friend and first cousin, the now celebrated "RLS", I must try to say something – hardly more perhaps than a few words. My knowledge of him, though long and deep, cannot be conveyed by words.'

Then after a brief, anodyne reminiscence about Louis at a family wedding, Katharine moved on to North Berwick where, as her father lay paralysed at Anchor House, she had played on the sands with Louis and Bob, the two most important people in her life: 'No other men nor other women were ever quite to me what these two were and remained.' For the record, and carefully avoiding any suggestion of impropriety, she mentioned her travels as a runaway wife in France with Louis and Snoodie. Then finally came the precious time in Bournemouth when she had felt closest to her cousin since his marriage to someone else: 'It was at Bournemouth he one morning told me of a dream which crystallised into his *Jekyll and Hyde*. This book, dedicated to me, with verses and a letter in his own writing, is in the presentation copy still in my possession. Our long alliance was broken for ever by his departure for the South Seas; but while I live my memories of him live too.'

### AVE!

#### Dedicated to Katharine de Mattos

Bells upon the city are ringing in the night;
High above the gardens are the houses full of light;
On the heathy Pentlands is the curlew flying free;
And the broom is blowing bonnie in the north countrie.

We cannae break the bonds that God decreed to bind,
Still we'll be the children of the heather and the wind;
Far away from home, O, it's still for you and me
That the broom is blowing bonnie in the north countrie!

# Further Reading

ROBERT LOUIS STEVENSON was his own best biographer, leaving behind nearly 3,000 letters brought together in the eight-volume Yale University Press edition through the painstaking efforts of Ernest Mehew, to whom all Stevensonians owe an incalculable debt. To enjoy some of the best, try the one-volume *Selected Letters of Robert Louis Stevenson* (Yale 1997).

Any Stevenson biographer stands on the shoulders of a tall totem pole of predecessors, to all of whom I am indebted. The first, Stevenson's cousin Graham Balfour (*The Life of Robert Louis Stevenson*, 1901) did most of the heavy lifting, albeit under the watchful eye of Stevenson's widow. Since then many have added more detail. For the most recent full-length biography, try *Robert Louis Stevenson* by Claire Harman (HarperCollins, 2005).

A host of living memories of RLS, including a tantalisingly brief contribution by Katharine de Mattos, were gathered on behalf of the Robert Louis Stevenson Club by Rosaline Masson in 1922. They range from a San Francisco shop assistant's banal recollection of a 12-word conversation with the *Jekyll and Hyde* author – 'You're a Scotsman aren't you?' 'Yes.' 'Where are you from?' 'Aberdeenshire.' 'Ah!' – to the most beautiful, vivid and detailed memories recalled by Rosaline's sister Flora. Second-hand copies of *I Can Remember Robert Louis Stevenson* (1922) are easy to find, or download the text free from the Internet Archive.

The most comprehensive RLS online resource can be found at a website run by Edinburgh Napier University: www.robert-louis-stevenson.org. It offers free downloadable versions of most of Stevenson's works.

The world is fascinated by lighthouses and lighthouse builders, and Stevensons' relatives were not shy of proclaiming their achievements. Robert Stevenson and his son Alan, Katharine's father, both wrote accounts of the building of the Bell Rock lighthouse off Arbroath, while Alan told how he built the much bigger Skerryvore lighthouse off Scotland's stormy west coast. RLS drew on these to write his *Records of a Family of Engineers*. The best and most readable modern account is *The Lighthouse Stevensons* by Bella Bathhurst (HarperCollins 1999).

A copy of the original 1865 edition of Katharine's father's *Ten Hymns of Synesius and Some Occasional Pieces* – including 'Manuela the Mountain Maid' – is in the National Library of Scotland and the text can be downloaded free via its online catalogue.

*Black Bess or The Knight of the Road, A Tale of the Good Old Times* by Edward Viles, was a penny dreadful running for 254 issues from 1863, now downloadable free from the Internet Archive.

As one of the first independent women working as journalists in Victorian Britain, Katharine features in *Their Fair Share: Women, Power and Criticism in The Athenaeum*, by Marysa Demoor (Routledge, 2000).

Katharine's brother Bob – the art critic RAM Stevenson – hated writing and his *Engraving, a Translation from La Gravure of Vicomte H Delaborde* (1886) is mainly the work of his sister. He did manage to produce *The Art of Velasquez* (1895), still regarded as an important work on the Spanish artist, but it contains none of Bob's brilliantly entertaining monologues, which died with him. For a flavour of these we must rely on the memory of his friend HG Wells, who put one such monologue in the mouth of the artist Bob Ewart in his novel *Tono-Bungay* (1909).

The life of Walter Ferrier's 'honoured father', including the disreputable disease that ended it, is laid bare in *Ferrier of St Andrews: An Academic Tragedy* by Arthur Thomson (1985).

The life of the burly, bearded, one-legged man on whom RLS based Long John Silver is chronicled in *WE Henley* by John Connell (1949). Henley's sincere affection for the friend he addressed as 'My dear Louis' can be seen in *The Letters of William Ernest Henley to Robert Louis Stevenson*, ed. Damian Atkinson (Rivendale Press, 2008).

To read Beggars and Stevenson's other well-paid contributions to *Scribner's Magazine* in their original form, along with The Nixie that appeared under Fanny's byline, download them free from Cornell University's Making of America searchable online collection.

The sex-crazed socialist career of William Sydney de Mattos as a Fabian prophet of free love is perhaps mercifully shrouded in mystery. A little can be gleaned from *Educate, Agitate, Organize, 100 Years of Fabian Socialism*, by Patricia Pugh (1984).

For more on Katharine and Louis's family try *Memoirs of a Soldier's Daughter* by Susan Miles (Ursula Wyllie Roberts), downloadable free from wyllie.org.nz.

For more on Richardson Fowke, Katharine's bigamous and abusive Jekyll and Hyde brother-in-law, visit the excellent fooksfamily.com genealogy website which has information gathered by Dora Stevenson's great-grandson Dicky Wallis.

# **Luath** Press Limited

*committed to publishing well written books worth reading*

LUATH PRESS takes its name from Robert Burns, whose little collie Luath (*Gael.*, swift or nimble) tripped up Jean Armour at a wedding and gave him the chance to speak to the woman who was to be his wife and the abiding love of his life. Burns called one of the 'Twa Dogs' Luath after Cuchullin's hunting dog in Ossian's *Fingal*.
Luath Press was established in 1981 in the heart of Burns country, and is now based a few steps up the road from Burns' first lodgings on Edinburgh's Royal Mile. Luath offers you distinctive writing with a hint of unexpected pleasures.
Most bookshops in the UK, the US, Canada, Australia, New Zealand and parts of Europe, either carry our books in stock or can order them for you. To order direct from us, please send a £sterling cheque, postal order, international money order or your credit card details (number, address of cardholder and expiry date) to us at the address below. Please add post and packing as follows: UK – £1.00 per delivery address; overseas surface mail – £2.50 per delivery address; overseas airmail – £3.50 for the first book to each delivery address, plus £1.00 for each additional book by airmail to the same address. If your order is a gift, we will happily enclose your card or message at no extra charge.

**Luath** Press Limited
543/2 Castlehill
The Royal Mile
Edinburgh EH1 2ND
Scotland
Telephone: +44 (0)131 225 4326 (24 hours)
email: sales@luath. co.uk
Website: www. luath.co.uk